SHEILA .ted at
her local convent school. She attended Dublin's College of
Catering and UCD before going on to lecture in Marketing
in Senior College, Dún Laoghaire. She is married to her
childhood sweetheart, Irish historian and author Diarmaid
Ferriter, and has three young children. She has been a
regular contributor to *Sunday Miscellany* on RTÉ Radio 1
and is currently on a career break to look after her children
and concentrate on her writing. *Six at the Table* is her
first book.

Six at the Table

Sheila Maher

·THE·
BLACK·
·STAFF·
PRESS

First published in 2011 by
Blackstaff Press
4c Heron Wharf, Sydenham Business Park
Belfast, BT3 9LE
with the assistance of
The Arts Council of Northern Ireland

Typeset by CJWT Solutions, St Helens, Merseyside

Printed in Great Britain by the MPG Books Group

A CIP catalogue record for this book
is available from the British Library

ISBN 978 0 85640 869 4

www.blackstaffpress.com

*To my
mother and father*

Clockwise from left: Dad, Catherine, Mum, Me, Kevin
and Lucy, August 1978

Contents

Prologue

As my feet hit the cold kitchen floor I wish I had remembered to put on socks. I shiver as I fill the kettle and stand hugging myself tightly, waiting for it to boil. I stare out the window and can just make out the black and bare outline of trees in the back garden. It is still dark outside – there isn't even a hint of dawn breaking in the distance. I know I looked at my watch only a minute or two ago, but I've already forgotten what time it is – it's very early, of that I'm sure.

I look around at the mess in the kitchen and try to forget all of the work that still has to be done to make this home habitable. How could everything have changed so completely in one short year?

Our postal code has increased by ten, our mortgage has doubled, our income has halved, we have two gardens instead of one. Our sex life has quartered – then quartered again. Instead of eight hours' sleep, I'm lucky if I get five. Instead of several nights out a week, we can barely drag ourselves out for one. We are three instead of two.

Only the briefest while ago I used to pity the two-car, two-kid suburbanites whose days seemed so dull and routine. I would wonder how and why people chose to exist like that, while we were really living!

I can hear her cries getting more insistent, so I will the kettle along. As it comes to the boil I pour the bubbling water around the bottle and make my way upstairs. My legs are heavy and my back stiff – they could do with another hour or two of rest. I glance at our bedroom door and think of my side of the bed – still warm and snug with my shape pressed into it, and a fuzzy heat emanating from him. Unfortunately I'm not going to be able to take up that position again for some time.

I open the door to her bedroom and immediately the crying stops and instead her legs and arms start flapping excitedly. As I look into the cot a broad gummy smile cracks on her face. My insides swell to bursting point. Is it me or the anticipation of her bottle that has her so happy? I reach in to pick her up. *This* is my favourite part of the day. This is when I reacquaint myself with her wriggling body and gorgeous smell. This is life.

I sit down on the bed and, holding her in my arms, I start to feed her. She sucks methodically and contentedly. I close my eyes and feel them sting beneath my hot lids. My mind drifts off. I think of my mother doing this same thing almost forty years ago. I think of her holding me tightly and tenderly in this nurturing embrace. I think of all the toil and the feedings that are involved in rearing, not one but four children. How many bottles did she warm? How many tonnes of food did she purée and mash and blend for us as babies? How many thousand dinners did she lovingly prepare for us to enjoy? How many hours of her life did she spend standing at her workspace in our kitchen? My mother grew old standing in our kitchen, I see that now. I see too with a hint of regret, mixed with a pinch of anticipation, that I now seem to be heading down that well-worn path.

The Kitchen

It was 1979 and I was nine years old, the second youngest child in a family of six. My world was small and at its centre was our house – a sturdy, block-like 1960s semi in South Dublin. A big square box containing all our living quarters, with a smaller square box – the garage – on the side. Our garage was attached to that of our neighbours, which in turn was attached to their house, and so on down the half-moon of the Crescent, up the Rise, into the Park, around the Grove and back along the Avenue. Each house was the mirror image, maybe slightly altered over time, of the one opposite and a carbon copy of the one next door. There was white pebbledash plaster on the top of our house and red brick on the bottom – it was only half a red brick.

My parents spent the first two years of married life in a one-bedroom flat until they had the deposit saved. They loved to tell, and for some strange reason we enjoyed hearing, how they moved in with nothing but a bed, two borrowed chairs and a small card table, plus a new baby – Catherine, my big sister – in a cot. The four of us children gazed on as they told us in unison how they saved for a sofa, put a deposit on a fridge and how Dad did most of the other work himself. They each gazed into the middle distance as they recalled those years, as if the images were projected into the space above our dinner table and only they could see them. We hung on to every word as they spoke tenderly of life 'before us'. Their change of manner with each other during these moments was more of a revelation to me than the story I had heard several times before. Such vague and minute displays of affection between my parents were welcome – they seldom kissed in front of us. Though there were times when Mum would make an exaggerated leap for Dad and smother him in kisses, which he would then swat away in playful mock-horror. She would do this, I knew, as a form of reassurance for us, as much as for her own pleasure.

At the end of these musings one of them, usually Mum, would declare their exasperation at how young people today had to have everything in place before they moved into their new homes. The inference, understood through their tut-tuts and pursed lips, was that young people, the ranks of which I hoped to someday join, were soft nowadays; they suffered some weakness of character or lack of backbone, because they chose not to live in unfurnished, unheated and undecorated accommodation.

The front door of our house opened into a large square hallway. The floor was covered in a chocolate brown carpet with a tight pattern of faint cream and green swirls and concentric circles all over it – such carpets didn't show up the dirt, Mum said. The walls were a vibrant egg-yolk yellow. To the left were the stairs going up. To the right was the door to the sitting room; a rarely used dining room lay beyond this. Straight ahead was the kitchen. The nerve centre. The hub. The heart.

It was a large kitchen. Square also. My parents were pleased to inform anyone who asked, particularly neighbours, how they had had the wherewithal to pay a little extra to the builder when buying off the plans to shorten the hallway by a few feet, thereby enlarging the kitchen by a vital amount. They were savvy in their own unassuming way and proud of it.

Opposite the entrance was a large window overlooking a generous back garden. The garden was south-facing, so the kitchen was almost always flooded with bright sunlight. Beneath the window on the left was the sink, on the right was the electric cooker, and in between the two was a countertop, with some presses underneath. This was where Mum spent most of her days. This was her production line. She moved from sink to cooker to countertop, then back to cooker. The flow of movement only changed if she had to go to the small fridge on the opposite wall or to the freezer in the garage. It was only rarely that I walked into that kitchen and did not see Mum's back as she stirred a pot on the hob or peeled some potatoes at the sink.

The right-hand wall of the kitchen held all the presses and more counter space. Dad made all of the units himself, along with most of the furniture in our house – carpentry and DIY being his only hobbies. A proud craftsman, he never rushed a job or cut corners – measure twice, cut once, he told me, passing on his words of wisdom as I patiently watched him laying his inch-tape across a plank of wood for the fifth time. The doors of the presses were made of the thinnest plywood and painted pure white, with arched white plastic handles – they gave a sharp click each time they were opened and closed. They received an annual painting to keep them looking respectable. The wall-mounted presses above held all the cups, glasses and plates. The ones beneath held saucepans, bowls and lots of dry goods. As a small child, I sat for hours on the kitchen floor as Mum worked around me. I took out and examined the opened and half-used packets of flour, sugar, ground almonds, icing sugar, tubes of tomato purée, bottles of Worcestershire sauce, vinegar, and Irel coffee, asking Mum what each one was, playing 'shop', and making her buy them all back from me. I was amazed that she could tell apart the identical jam jars of bread soda, baking powder, Bextartar and salt. They all looked the same to me.

The left wall was unencumbered by fixtures and fittings, as our table was pushed against it when not in use. It was the only wall in the kitchen with wallpaper – an inoffensive pale peach colour – yet it was continually covered in pictures and posters. It became over time an informal 'educational' space. It always had a large map of the world in the centre, stuck on with Blu-Tack and beside that, for many years, was the annual Mitchelstown calendar – a poster-sized calendar with a photograph of an agricultural scene depicting cows, green pastures and blue skies on the top, the twelve months of the years on the bottom, and a large hamper of cheeses, yoghurts and milk spread out across the middle. Postcards from friends and relatives who travelled Ireland and abroad filled any gaps.

For a long time a height chart filled the last free space on this wall and over the years we logged our progression upwards. I flew up that chart with frightening rapidity. When we had all soared above the top and it had lost its use, Dad replaced it with an anti-drugs chart he brought home from his office in the Eastern Health Board. Aimed at teenagers and their parents, it was part of a campaign to inform, educate, but primarily to scare youngsters away from ever trying drugs. This chart used colours to represent the level of danger that each drug posed, starting with pale yellow for alcohol and tobacco, getting a hint more orange for hash and grass, and moving on into bright orange and red with explicit details of how cocaine, heroin and crack cocaine can affect your body and mind. I studied this chart closely and wondered if I would become the kind of teenager brave enough to try such bizarre substances. I tried to imagine what 'hallucinations', 'trips' and 'psychotic episodes' were. Then this chart disappeared overnight. Dad was unsure if giving us so much information was not actually encouraging us to experiment in some way. Cuttings from the newspaper about switching lights off to save money and Lenten campaign posters showing small black children with flies on their lips made their way onto this space instead.

The back wall of the kitchen was where the small fridge was plugged in. Beside it was a wing chair and Mum's trolley. An engagement present, this trolley was gold and had two levels. It was only used for visitors, when it was wheeled into the sitting room, looking like a cross between a stately pram and a tea-lady's trolley. The top tier would be laden with rattling cups and saucers, sugar and milk and, hidden under an oversized tea cosy which Mum had crocheted, sat the teapot. Plates of sandwiches, shortbread biscuits and a flan filled with fresh cream and tinned pears, with a dusting of sugar on top, crowded the bottom shelf.

We ate most of our meals in the kitchen. Only on rare occasions were we allowed to eat in front of the television in the sitting room: Wimbledon – semi-finals and finals – or when Jimmy Connors was playing (Mum never missed a Connors match); Christmas night, eating turkey sandwiches and Lemon's sweets, while watching *The Sound of Music* or *Some Like it Hot*; breakfast cereal in front of *Swap Shop* on Saturday mornings.

The kitchen was the room from which I heard muffled shouts and raised voices in my bedroom at night. Trying to sleep and to listen at the same time, I'd hear Dad's bellows and Mum's shrill tones rise through the floor from the kitchen below. They'd be sitting at the table talking loudly. I'd hear one of them walk out to the garage and slam the door, only to walk back in seconds later and shout again. I'd hear fast footsteps on the stairs and their bedroom door shutting gently but firmly as their voices went quiet. Then I'd drift off, only to wonder as I opened my eyes to daylight what the atmosphere would be like in the kitchen that following morning.

The kitchen was where we children also took our fights when we were looking for a referee. When Catherine and Lucy cut the beautiful blond hair off my Sindy doll, it was into the kitchen to Mum that I went running and sobbing, holding that less-than-ideal image of womanhood in my small hands. When Lucy borrowed Catherine's favourite Benetton green-and-white-striped cotton 'rugby shirt', they both stormed into the kitchen to see which of them was most justified in being hysterical – the borrower or the borrowee. When Kevin cursed for the first time in front of

Dad and was dragged up to his bedroom for punishment, once again it was into the kitchen that I ran crying, looking for comfort from Mum.

We washed, slept and relaxed in the other rooms of our symmetrical box, but it was in the kitchen that we lived.

Picnics On The Beach

Throughout the summer months we watched the weekend evening news religiously – to get the weather forecast. The news itself was half watched as Dad read his newspaper and Mum flitted around the kitchen, popping her head in every now and then to see what she was missing. When the weather forecast was announced, Dad put the paper to rest on his stomach and, with her rubber gloves still on, Mum stood in silence at the door, staring intently at the screen. Any signs of high pressure, isobars spread far apart and a capital H in the centre, and we, like thousands of other families, made our way to the seaside in Wicklow. There was a sense of urgency about getting a 'good day' on the beach – a day without rain, a day we could treasure during the long winter months ahead. The merest suggestion of temperatures topping the high teens was enough to make Mum and Dad organise a Saturday by the sea.

The weather that summer did not disappoint, and it was with great excitement one Friday evening that Mum and Dad told us that we were heading to Wicklow for the last beach trip of the season. I got up quite early – as I always did on beach days – and put on my favourite sundress, the one with tiny red love hearts all over it. The straps tied together to make a neat little bow on each shoulder, and the beads which dangled from their ends would clack together noisily as I ran. When I entered the kitchen, I saw by the amount of work Mum had already done that she'd probably been there since sunrise. Tall, with a broad back, she had a sensible kind of frame for a mother of four. Her greying hair was completely flat on one side from her night's sleep, though later she would dampen and vigorously brush her thick wiry curls, pressing errant strands back into place in front of the bathroom mirror. This she did every day. The belt of her dusty pink dressing gown was tied tightly around her middle and her dry and cracked heels were spilling over the back of her slippers. She'd covered the kitchen table with cups, flasks and sandwich parcels and she greeted me without turning around or stopping her work. I was given brusque instructions to eat my breakfast and then waken Dad and tell him he had to pack the car.

It took a few hours to get us all up and ready, then we squeezed into our laden Opel Kadett and crawled out on to the main road south, the N11, joining the long queue of cars shunting in the same direction; a parched snake heading slowly for the coast. Magheramore beach, on the outskirts of Wicklow town, was our family's 'secret' beach. Mum and Dad heard of it in hushed tones from a colleague of Dad's nine summers before, when Mum was heavily pregnant with me. From that day onwards they rarely went to another beach. Brittas Bay and the Silver Strand were visited only occasionally, as Magheramore had stolen our hearts. It lay at the end of a narrow and bumpy dirt track where branches slapped you in the face if you left the car window open – which I did for the thrill of it. Deep potholes tested the suspension of Dad's overburdened car.

The limited parking at the end of the lane was haphazard –
you might get your car in but you were never guaranteed you
would be able to get it out, as more and more Dubliners
squeezed into the small field throughout the day. Dad usually
left our car on the grass verge by the side of the lane, pointing
outwards for ease of exit. With the car tilted at an angle, and
the two left wheels suspended over a ditch, we all shuffled out
the safe side. Then out of the boot came the togs bag – an old
plastic compost bag holding six towels and many more pairs
of togs – two tennis racquets; tennis balls and beach balls; a
Frisbee; two large chequered rugs; two plastic bags full of food;
a windbreak; and a bag with Dad's newspaper and camera. All
of this had to make its way down a steep and slippery slope to
the beach. Dad carried most of it, over his back, under his
arms, in both hands, strapped across his shoulders, while the
rest of us carried a token ball or rug. Mum was always terrified
of slipping and twisting her ankle so she used a tennis racquet
as a crutch to help her down. She would snap at Dad if,
unchivalrously, he left her too far behind and she grew
embarrassed if a stranger offered to help her down – Dad
would always get an earful later.

As soon as my feet sank in the soft shifting sand, I ran
ahead to see if 'our' spot was free. If another family ever had
the audacity to spread their rug in our place, I would give
them my most withering look and then try to find the next
best location, one that was equidistant from all the other
families and would meet with everyone's approval.

On the beach my priorities were to swim and eat;
Catherine (fourteen) wanted to get a tan; Lucy (twelve)
wanted to swim too; and Kevin (seven) wanted to stay sand-

free. So as soon as our rugs were laid out and Dad had pounded our windbreak into the sand to mark our patch for the day, I stripped off, put on my togs and plunged into the icy Irish Sea.

Regardless of how grey or blue the sky and water were, whether there were exciting waves or just a gentle lilt to the sea, Lucy and I, as the water babies of the family, would walk at a steady pace straight up to our waists and then dive under for several seconds to wet our heads and shoulders – this time was no different. As the first to get wet, we were greeted with a loud cheer when we resurfaced, both satisfaction and pain clearly visible on our faces. Kevin somewhat reluctantly waded in after us; he was not that happy about being forced in for a swim, nor did he want to be associated with Catherine, shivering in her first bikini in two inches of water. Mum's approach was to glide into the water with a breaststroke that would have been graceful had it not been for a loud spurting of water – looking and sounding as if it had come from a blocked hose – that came out of her mouth on each upward stroke. Dad was the only one to enter the water backwards. He stood with his back to the horizon and the oncoming waves, stretched out his arms like a scarecrow and made big circles with them as he collapsed back into the trustworthy water behind him. We each had our own entry style but Catherine's was the most tortuous. By the time we had all splashed around, played D-O-N-K-E-Y with the beach ball and practised some swimming, Catherine had turned grey in the shallows, goose bumps all over. Bored pleading with her to get under, Dad and Kevin started splashing and chasing her to make

her topple and fall in. As she fell, my chattering teeth told me to get out. Catherine ended up swimming alone.

It took a while to get warm again; this I did under the cover of the towelling robe. Mum made one for each of us girls – to protect our modesty. She'd got a long piece of towelling, threaded elastic around the top and then stitched the ends together. The elastic stayed around my neck as the towel hung down, covering my body from the gaze of onlookers. I liked being naked under that private tent, the air drying the salt water from my skin and the sand from my bottom. I then put on dry togs and reappeared from under my robe, placing my wet togs on the rocks to dry. Dad shook out the rugs and Mum arranged the picnic.

First out were the sandwiches. There were several parcels, each one wrapped in the saved waxed paper of previously eaten loaves. Most popular were the ham sandwiches, made with white bread and a thick layer of butter. There were rounds of cheese sandwiches made with pale slices of the only cheese we knew, Calvita. Protected in its small cardboard box and foil wrapping, an entire block was required for our picnic. There were egg sandwiches, now soggy and misshapen, with a little chopped chive, made with brown bread. Just for Mum, there were the more elegant cheese and apple sandwiches. She offered to share them with us but had no takers. Why did she put a nice crisp apple into a perfectly good cheese sandwich and ruin both of them? Obviously an acquired taste. The sandwiches never ran out no matter how many we ate. But before they were even half eaten, Mum took out some home-made fruit scones, which she had buttered that morning. All of this was washed down with diluted orange drink for us kids, poured from a large Tupperware container into plastic cups. Chilled in the fridge before we left home, this drink was by now tepid, which spoiled its usually enjoyable thirst-quenching properties. Mum and Dad preferred real mugs for their tea, which they made with their flask of hot water, and with tea bags, sugar and milk kept separately in used Coleman's Mustard jars. No picnic would be complete without a final treat of some kind and ours was usually Mum's flapjacks or queen cakes.

On many occasions we were joined on the beach by close friends and extended family, those in the know with regards to its location. Aunty Mary from England, and her husband and sons, would join us if they were in Ireland on a visit. Aunty Eileen and my only girl cousin Jean often made it down the treacherous slopes to join us too. So did our neighbours, the Devitts. The ages of the Devitt children were such that a convenient pairing of sorts took place. During

these days more chequered rugs were spread out and picnics very similar to our own were devoured. I strained to see what goodies were pulled from their bags and shamelessly hovered nearby in the hope of being offered a spare biscuit or some extra cake.

With more people around, there was more sport to be had once the food was gone. We would run off our lunch by playing a personalised version of cricket or rounders, using a tennis racquet, tennis ball and balled-up jumpers as bases or stumps. The games were dumbed-down to ensure that Kevin and I, as the youngest, stood a chance of hitting the ball. On several occasions Mum or Aunty Mary sprained their ankle running from jumper to jumper around the pitch, bringing the games to an abrupt halt.

I loved the last swim of the day. By four in the afternoon, and after many swims, I'd be used to the cold water, and it didn't wind me on entry. I stayed in for as long as I could, until Mum shouted for me to get dressed, it was time to go home. Though this really meant it was time for a last mini-picnic before we started the trek back up the slope.

This was when the 'shop stuff' came out: a litre and a half of Club Orange, a six pack of Tayto crisps, a family pack of Fox's Glacier Fruits or Ritchie's Milky Moos to suck on the hike back to the car. The taste of the sand and the sea were washed away by the bubbles and salt of this picnic, making me forget the sand itching in my knickers and my matted wet hair as I licked cheesy fingers and tipped the crisp packet into my mouth to get all those tiny salty crumbs out of the corners. I loudly sucked on as many boiled sweets as I was given as I trudged my way back along the now busy beach, full of windbreaks and rugs and families, sprawled out, shouting, eating, running, splashing, chasing, and sunbathing. I'd feel momentarily sad when I turned around from my vantage point at the top of the slope and took one last look at the wonderful scene below. I hated leaving the beach behind.

Sometimes we stopped for ice creams on the way home. This treat was Dad's prerogative – the gift was either bestowed upon us or not, and I never dared to ask outright for an ice cream. The not knowing if we were to stop or not kept me alert in the sticky car, fighting the temptation to doze off. I was anxious not to miss Rathnew – the last place in Wicklow that Dad would stop. Silently my heart would sink if the car kept going past the tiny grocery shop on the right. Sometimes the indicator tick-tocked, the car slowed down and Dad pulled in to the side of the road. A few minutes later he'd return with a delicious selection of ice creams. Gollybar for Mum, Choc Ice for himself, and a mixed bag for us to fight over. There'd be the stale crumbliness of a Brunch, a sweet, tangy Orange Split, a Loop the Loop and another Gollybar. We'd snatch at them quickly – any one of them was welcome and each had its own attraction. I was always particularly happy to be left with the simple softness of the unadorned Gollybar.

After sucking the wooden stick dry to remove the slightest trace of ice cream, I'd doze off in the car, utterly content. Hot from the sunburn already glowing crimson on my cheeks and shoulders, I'd feel damp and gritty and smell clean and dirty at the same time. So deliciously tired. Only waking as I sensed, somewhere in my core, the familiar swing of the car turning up our road.

Strawberries

PLEASE DON'T EAT THE FRUIT was the most ineffectual sign that was ever ignored. It hung on the gate at the entrance to the field in Malahide where we went strawberry-picking. It was incredibly naïve of the farmer to assume we would obey it.

I was given a green cardboard box, pointed in the direction of the day's beds and told to get picking. It took a while to get used to crouching and bending but I'd soon get into my own rhythm: one for the box, one for me, one for the box, one for me. I stopped caring that I was getting muck on my bare knees and in between my toes and under my toenails. Initially, sibling rivalry worked to my parents' advantage as we each tried to fill our boxes the fastest. I'd thrill when I brushed aside a few leaves to find a cluster of strawberries that previous pickers had missed. Glossy red and luxuriant, they huddled together, as if knowingly hiding from greedy fingers. It took a lot of willpower for me to place any of them in my box.

Mum preferred to pick, and eat, raspberries. She'd set off into the next field, claiming it was easier on her back. Dad usually kept close to her and left us kids down at ground level with the strawberries. Once our bounty was weighed and paid for, Dad lined the boot of the car with neat rows of boxes, and I spent the long journey home from Malahide wondering if I'd have fresh cream or ice cream with my strawberries after dinner.

But before they could be enjoyed, the fruit had to be weighed, washed, divided, bagged, refrigerated, and left aside to be frozen or preserved. It was a military operation, and one in which I was fully enlisted. Some of the berries were laid out flat on trays and frozen for use in desserts to brighten up dark winter days. A smaller consignment was set aside for immediate consumption, with some to be given to friends and Grandma. The majority were fated to become Mum's luscious sweet jam.

She'd take two industrial-sized saucepans, kept solely for this purpose, from the back of a cupboard and fetch from the garage the dozen empty jam jars. Then she weighed mountains of white sugar. With the potato masher, she bashed and squashed our beautiful strawberries into a runny pulp before she turned on the heat and started to cook them. The fierce bubbling and vigorous splashing of the molten lumpy liquid was scary to watch and I'd be ordered to stand well back from the cooker. Mum stirred and waited, stirred and paused, stirred and stared unblinking into the pot, as if expecting a sign to appear on the surface. Now and then she lifted the wooden spoon out and scrutinised the back of that too. I felt tense. I knew there was a lot riding on this. If Mum called it too early and potted the jam before its time, she would pour it all back into the saucepan and start again. She did this once before and never let herself forget it. However, if she waited too long and let the jam overcook, as she had done last summer, there was no way of repairing the damage. All winter long when each jam jar popped open, she would shake her head, heave and sigh, 'What a waste – what a disaster!', as we dug our knives into the solid mass of dark red jam and tried to spread it without tearing our bread to pieces. This year Mum got it right. At the end of the afternoon, clustered together on the kitchen table and only distinguishable upon close inspection, were half a dozen jars each of strawberry jam and raspberry jam. The jars still hot to the touch – their colours rich and tantalising.

The best job of the day was dividing the berries that had been spared from the freezer or jam jar into six portions for dessert. I very carefully counted each berry into the six bowls to ensure equity and fairness. I even allowed for size differences and compensated the bowls with the smaller berries. When I finished, I stood back and admired my work – each bowl looked identical, no one could complain of being short-changed. Even so, I knew which bowl I was going to pick. We got to choose between ice cream or fresh cream as an accompaniment. A bit of both was best.

Pasta?

Mum had been working up to it for a long time. She had discussed it with Aunty Mary in London, who did it weekly and loved it; she had cut out and pored over articles about it in the newspaper and women's magazines; and she had a fair idea of how to go about it. She was ready to try something new. She was gathering courage to tackle the world of Italian cuisine. She was going to make her first spaghetti bolognese.

Used to preparing stews, Mum found the meat sauce easy to make – all the simpler for her as she had to leave out the garlic in order to spare her husband's flavour-sensitive digestive tract. She took her time with it, double-checking her recipe before adding bacon, a tin of tomatoes, a pinch – or was it a teaspoonful? – of mixed herbs to the pot.

Unfamiliar smells filled the kitchen that Saturday afternoon as Mum delighted herself by being so adventurous. After thirty minutes of simmering, the sauce deepened in colour to a lavish red. I was looking forward to tasting this dinner. My understanding of spaghetti came from *Lady and the Tramp* – the romantic scene where the two dogs share a bowl of pasta, each starting at opposite ends of a long string of spaghetti until their mouths touch in a sort of kiss. Or from watching Americans on our television screen devour large forkfuls of tightly wound spaghetti. It looked like fun. I wanted to try it.

I didn't offer any assistance to Mum as she banged around the kitchen. Somehow I knew that when preparing a whole new food group for the first time, she was better left alone. I waited for the call to the table instead. When it came, I was taken aback to see each dinner plate piled high with bolognese sauce atop an even larger mound of white rice. I looked from plate to plate not quite understanding if I was mistaken and rice was indeed pasta.

'Emmm.' I hesitated. 'Is there not meant to be some kind of stringy spaghetti with this?'

'You're having rice with it today,' Mum retorted. 'It'll be easier to eat this way.'

Disappointed and robbed of a chance to finally taste pasta, I forked the 'rice bolognese' into my mouth. There was no loud sucking required, no messy splashing as threads of pasta, slick with tomato sauce, swung back and stained my clothes, no large mouthfuls that wound expertly around my fork as I twirled it round and round on my plate. Instead, I ate easily and cleanly through my tasty but boring bolognese. Everyone asked for seconds, and Mum was visibly thrilled with herself. Even Dad ate a plateful without complaining of 'wild' flavours and potential indigestion. She wondered out loud why she had waited so long to try it.

When I stood up at the end of the meal to leave my plate at the sink, I spotted the problem. Down in the sink, hidden from view, sat the spaghetti. It had not separated during cooking. A congealed snake of pasta, as thick as my arm, curled into itself. As it cooled, it had glued itself firmly to the bottom of Mum's colander.

From that evening on, when Mum said we were having spaghetti bolognese for dinner, she meant rice. She didn't like to make such big blunders in the kitchen, and she didn't like the waste of good food that had to be thrown out, so she let considerable time elapse before she gave pasta a second try.

.

Salad

Some summer days Mum took a break from the heat of the kitchen and decided that a salad would be 'nice 'n' easy'. I liked to help out on salad days. Maybe it was the lack of hot surfaces and bubbling saucepans that made Mum relax and enjoy having a helper in her kitchen.

She prepared all the fancy salads herself: coleslaw, potato salad, and her own personal favourite, celery and apple salad. I was allowed to wash the lettuce and pat it dry on a clean tea towel, then divide it equally into neat piles on six dinner plates. Next, I picked the shells off three hard-boiled eggs, placed each one on the base of the egg-slicer and with great satisfaction guillotined it into seven or eight slices. Mum cut the tomatoes so thinly she only needed two tomatoes between six of us. I arranged an equal amount of egg, tomato and cucumber on each pile of lettuce, with perhaps a tiny bit more on Dad's. Next up was the meat, usually leftover ham or chicken. Mum divided this herself, as she knew who was to get white or brown meat – she did her best to honour our preferences on leftover days too. Then while she chopped scallions over everyone's salad, I got the fancy serving tray from the sitting room. Into each of the four smoked-glass dishes fitted in the tray, I spooned Mum's prepared salads, some beetroot if it was on offer, and any leftover egg and tomato. This was the table's centrepiece, and with a few serving spoons, we could help ourselves. A basket filled to the brim with home-made brown bread and some white sliced pan was placed alongside it. Heinz Salad Cream was the last to arrive to the table. It bothered Mum that she hadn't decanted it into a serving bowl, as her upbringing dictated, but at some point during all of these preparations her enthusiasm waned and she gave in to this shortcut.

'Your dinner's getting cold!' was her witty cry to the table on salad days, and before long there were twelve arms going over and across, reaching, passing, grabbing, spooning, spreading and serving, amidst grunts and mutters of 'Want some?', 'Will I give you a spoon o' this?', 'Can I have a bit o' that?'. Colourful mounds were built up on each plate, surrounding the meat and lettuce Mum and I had prepared. There wasn't room on the table for six side plates for buttering our bread, so we shared three between us.

This was a meal that brought out the various personalities of each family member. Kevin chose to make one massive sandwich out of the entire contents of his plate. I looked on affectionately as he tried to get it into his mouth, with most of his filling sliding back onto his plate and down his T-shirt. Dad made numerous white bread sandwiches, each one plain and unadorned – one chicken, one egg, one salad, and so on, until his plate was cleared or until Mum mentioned he might get a heart attack if he ate any more white bread. I shared a side plate with Mum and gaped, incredulous, as she ate thick chunks of butter with some brown bread stuck to the back of it, as accompaniment to her salad. I found it difficult to swallow my lettuce and cucumber, which stuck in my throat no matter how many times I tried to gulp them down. In order to make it easier, I chopped everything on my plate into bite-sized pieces and mixed it all into one homogenous mass. Meat, celery and apple, cucumber, egg, lettuce – even the beetroot that turned the rest of my salad pink – got mixed together. It was a very democratic way of eating my dinner: nothing got priority; everything stood an equal chance of appearing on my fork at any given moment.

Mum felt she was depriving us in some way when she served up a salad; she was failing to perform her motherly duties adequately by not providing a hot meal. So with a salad there was always dessert. Usually apple tart and cream. Her tarts were unrivalled and were devoured by neighbours, friends and family – anyone who had ever been sick or unfortunate could be the lucky recipient of one of Mum's melt-in-the-mouth tarts. The pastry was buttery and light, the sweet apples still had just enough bite, and the dusting of sugar on top mixed well with the generous helping of whipped cream collapsing over it. Sublime.

Grace Before Meals

Along with an insatiable appetite, God was something Mum was anxious to pass on to her children. As soon as I could talk, I was helped to memorise prayers that I then recited nightly, kneeling by the side of my bed. Mum was a daily communicant; early morning, lunch time or evening, there was always a Mass she could attend and she worked her life around this. She kept an emergency rosary ring in a tiny pocket in her purse, just in case she was caught without her full set or was ever sitting still long enough to slip in a few quick decades. Otherwise she had her mother-of-pearl beads, which she kept in their small red leather purse and dangled from her hands over the pew during Mass. Wound around her fingers in a unique way, the beads passed through her fingers in a continuous loop. I never managed to master this and instead got my Holy Communion beads knotted and twisted around my hands. Prayer was even more present during Lent, when daily rosaries were foisted on us all.

We also said a prayer every evening before dinner. Religion may have had to take a back seat for breakfast, and lunch was a disparate affair, even at weekends, with each of us eating at different times, but for dinner we were all together, trapped in the kitchen. As we took our seats at the table, Mum was already chanting grace to the four walls, while she scurried around dishing out the food. We were expected to join in as her backing chorus. If a voice was inaudible, Mum threw a withering look in the direction from whence the silence came and instantly the decibels increased.

> Bless us, O Lord, as we sit together,
> Bless the food we eat today,
> Bless the hands that made the food,
> Bless us, O Lord.
> Amen.

No one dared to put a fork near a morsel of food until grace was over. Even Dad had to be seen to at least mouth the words or he got a scolding for being a bad example to us all.

There was no escape. Visitors were made to endure it too. They either joined in, mumbling, pretending to know the words, or they stared down at their plate of food in embarrassed silence as we intoned this special daily prayer.

Lilt

It was thanks to Mum's devotion to God that I found myself at a religious gathering in Kilkenny, where I experienced my first gastronomic epiphany.

On the off chance that God the Father, the Son and the Holy Ghost had passed us by unnoticed, she upped the ante on our religious practices and lured the entire family into joining a motley group of lay volunteers. Unaware of what was in store, we were welcomed into a religious movement called the Focolare. This benign group of holy people believed it was their duty to reach out and spread the love of God. We started to spend every second Sunday ensconced in houses in Rathfarnham, boys in one house, girls in another. I sat in a circle on the floor with a group of strangers – my sisters were in with the older girls – and we shared our experiences of God and how we 'thought of Jesus' in our daily lives: when we helped someone; didn't get angry; or did some good deed.

I never had an honest good deed to report. As the sharing moved around the circle from good girl to sweeter girl I begged my brain to get creative and come up with something, either a genuine memory or, as was usually the case, a falsehood conjured out of pure imagination. Most times my contribution was a modified and thinly disguised version of what someone else had shared. 'I thought of Jesus when I helped my granny carry her shopping home' and 'I thought of Jesus when I shared my scooter with my brother' were typically insipid and completely false offerings from me. The truth was that I never thought of Jesus, except when I was in a panic trying to make up a story about how I thought of Jesus.

I did not fit in at the Focolare. I was a fraud. I stayed very quiet. I spoke when spoken to, and sang in a hushed voice when folk-song practice was on. Even the pretty Filipina girl, who strummed enthusiastically at her guitar while we sang 'When You are in Our Midst' and 'Kumbaya, My Lord', could not entice me to the extra Masses and sing-songs that were held on alternate Sundays.

But Mum's enthusiasm was strong and she signed us up for a family retreat at a Focolare weekend in Kilkenny. Volunteers from around the country congregated to celebrate God, His love and their mission. We pitched our tent amidst the zealous and the good. Even *my* parents seemed to me to be racy rebels among this crowd of sandal-wearing, head-nodding and over-friendly missionaries. My Dad cursed occasionally, my Mum had been known to tell the odd smutty joke – out of my earshot of course – and they fought with each other. The other people around us were just too pleasant. Their smiles were too wide. I was distrustful and sceptical, for no other reason than their abiding niceness.

Most of the weekend went by in a blur of singing, praying and more singing. When not at Mass, we children spent time rehearsing songs and readings for the next Mass or prayer group. But there was time in our holy schedule for us to return to our tents to eat, and it was during one such break that my spiritual conversion occurred.

I was hanging around outside our tent, dragging my feet in the dry clay and kicking up dust in boredom, when Dad returned from the local shop with some fizzy drinks to be shared over our lunch. Three cans between six of us. He held a Club Orange, a Coke, and a new green-and-yellow can in his hands. I hovered at his elbow and 'bagsed' the new yellow drink before anyone else had a look in. Without waiting for food to arrive, I grabbed my glass. After several delicious sips, I tipped my head back and gulped down the remainder in one noisy swallow.

'What's it called?' I shouted to Dad.

'Lilt,' he said, examining the side of the can.

It was Lilt, and it was divine. The flavours of exotic fruits like pineapple and mango, which I'd heard of yet never tasted, seemed to have been squeezed and pressed tightly into my glass. I had never had anything so heavenly. The fact that it wasn't as fizzy as other drinks made it taste even sunnier and I could drink it faster, without getting the inside of my mouth stung from the fizz. From my first slug, I was a fan. Lilt left all other soft drinks half finished, going flat and lifeless in their large plastic bottles.

After lunch, my parents brought me back to my group and the final afternoon folk-song session. As they turned to leave me, the leader asked them if I would like to stay on at the retreat for two extra nights after their return to Dublin. I could stay in a dorm with the other girls and enjoy a special Mass.

Mum thought this an excellent idea: 'That'd be nice,

wouldn't it?' she said, beaming down at me.

I was seized by fear. I was already lonely at each of the singing and praying sessions. I disliked being away from my family. I most definitely did not want to be separated by what I imagined were hundreds of miles and many counties. We had been sold this weekend as a family holiday, which it clearly was not, and now I was to be left behind, all alone.

In front of a roomful of my peers, however, no matter how odious they were or how little I cared for them, I was not going to be a baby and cry. I wanted to look up at my parents and tell them that what I most desired was to leave this gathering behind, for all six of us to be squeezed into our old Opel Kadett and to get back to the life of a non-religious. It had already been a weekend of too much sincerity, an overdose of false piety, on my part, and I didn't think I could sustain the charade any longer. Instead, I just stood by while they agreed to hand me over for two more days.

'I've no clothes,' I whined quietly.

'Oh that's okay, I'm sure some of the others will share with you,' the group leader said.

'Where will I sleep?'

'There are plenty of spare beds in the girls' dorm,' she said helpfully.

Clearly I lacked the resources to come up with a clever enough roadblock that would get me away from the Focolare.

And just like that, the rest of my family packed away our tent and all our camping gear, and with more room than usual in the back seat of the car, they escaped back to Dublin, while I cried silently into my pillow each night.

Spare clothes weren't forthcoming. Perhaps they thought none of the girls had clothes to fit my wider girth, so I had to endure itching and scratching and the embarrassment of dirty clothes for two whole days, all the while trying to concentrate on singing and praying and not crying. The ultimate endurance test was the long car journey home, squeezed amidst the limbs of another family. A family with a different smell, no Foxes Glacier Fruits or Bon Bons, and a very quiet car.

When I finally got home, I didn't tell Mum and Dad about the rest of my stay in Kilkenny. I brushed over the details and displayed a remarkable bravado. I didn't hint at my loneliness and tried to remain blasé about my utter relief to be home. Instead of Jesus Christ and His Holy Spirit, all I brought back in my heart with me to Dublin was my new-found love of Lilt.

Picnic by the Side of the Road

We never found the lay-by on the road to Barley Cove.

'There's one after Cashel on the Cork side!' Dad chirped optimistically, leading us on and on without a break, in search of the elusive lay-by. It was August, and the car was hot and stuffy, but another forty miles sped by, with a lot of complaining and fighting in the back before Dad was instructed to pull in the next time he saw a 'safe place'.

We ate our picnic on the main Dublin–Cork road, on a grassy verge, three feet from speeding cars and articulated lorries. We huddled around the open boot, which was crammed with camping gear and suitcases. Mum had squeezed in the picnic bag at the edge for easy access. In it were the staples: ham sandwiches, egg sandwiches, scones and cakes. Surrounded by the noise of cars whizzing by at sixty miles an hour and trucks flinging dust and grit our way, we munched through round after round of sandwiches. At least it wasn't raining, because then we would have had to eat the picnic in the car, with windows fogging up from steaming teacups and damp breath.

Before we got back in the car, we peed by the side of the road as discreetly as we could, Mum holding her jacket

around each of us for privacy from the world at large. Then we continued on to West Cork.

We passed the time in the car playing 'I Spy', counting cars of different colours and making the alphabet from car registration plates and road signs. We got stuck at the letter Q and stared intently out the window willing the next Quinnsworth to come into view. But mostly we were bored and whinged at regular intervals, 'How many more miles? How many more miles?'

We arrived in Cork city late in the afternoon. Rain had been pounding noisily and ceaselessly on the hollow tin roof of Dad's car since Fermoy. Cork was a very big county, we were reminded; there was still a long way to go to get out West. We all brightened up on spotting a sign that said 'Goleen 15 miles'. As if on cue, a chorus of 'Goleen, Goleen, Go-lee-eee-een, I'm beggin' of you please don't take my man' broke out. These lyrics, stolen from that catchy Dolly Parton

number, were all we could remember and they were repeated for several miles until we tired of that game too.

Goleen, I knew, signified the ending of our journey and a few minutes after passing through it I saw the colours in the distance. Not the azure blue sea, or the kelly green fields, or grey and white cliffs, but the orange, reds and blues of tents pitched in the camp site. From our position on the sweep of road that led from Goleen to Barley Cove, I watched through the pouring rain as the tents came into focus, I saw the chaos of the camp site, and I strained my eyes to find a blank spot where we would pitch our tent and make our home for two whole weeks.

Chicken 'n' Chips

In the slanting August rain, Dad ran into the camp site office to pay his fee and get instructions for where we were to squeeze ourselves in. The heavy rain meant that we 'smaller' children got to stay in the relative warmth of the car with Mum while, in the dimming light with rain swiping at their faces, Dad and Catherine set up the trailer tent. This year, the new extension had to be added on to the original trailer, and from our snug position in the car, we heard Dad's cursing and Catherine snivelling and begging to be let back in beside us. But Dad needed her help and permission was refused. After several setbacks and collapses, the tent was ready. Dad lit a kerosene lamp, and from its place on the ground, it shed a warm light over the ubiquitous orange canvas. We sploshed across in its direction and stood inside the small space that was our new home. Despite the damp, the mud, and the even louder thudding of rain on the canvas roof, it seemed cosy.

The next task was unpacking and feeding. After a long day on the road, with only sandwiches and snacks to eat, Mum needed to get something warm and substantial inside us. And so the first things to be organised were the table, the table-top cooker and a couple of battered saucepans she kept for camping. The contents of a Tupperware container were spilled into a saucepan, and within a few minutes the beef stew Mum had prepared before we left Dublin was piping hot and ready to eat. She ladled it onto our waiting plastic plates, and even though I wasn't particularly hungry, I mopped up every spoonful. This dinner set the dietary balance straight. It recalibrated my system after a day of Foxes Glacier Mints, Hula Hoops, and sugary drinks. It set the tone for the holiday and reminded me what a pleasure it was to eat a hot dinner outdoors. It was like a picnic, only better.

Kevin and I succumbed to tiredness first. But before we could go to bed we had to trek across the camp site, with Dad guiding us by flashlight, to the bright toilets. We brushed our teeth, shivering while moths and dragonflies buzzed and pinged off the bare light bulbs above us. Back at the tent, I was glad to zip up my sleeping bag and cuddle up beside Kevin. I drifted off while the rest of the family sat only two feet and a few millimetres of canvas away from me, playing cards. I awoke the next morning with Lucy and Catherine fast asleep in their sleeping bags, their feet up beside my head and Kevin's. On the other side of the trailer Mum and Dad lay, their two sleeping bags zipped together.

Camping food was good but basic. The shop on site was expensive, so Mum and Dad did their best to avoid it. They'd brought as many provisions as they could pack from Dublin supermarkets and there was a preponderance of preserved and tinned foods. Tinned beans and peas were the main vegetables on offer, and after the first few days, when the fresh meat was finished, Spam salads featured prominently. But it was undoubtedly the night my parents threw caution

to the wind and ordered chicken 'n' chips from the on-site chipper that provided the best meal of the fortnight.

Kevin and I got our chance to get the dinner from the chipper because Catherine and Lucy had started hanging around with boys in the play area of the camp site. The instructions were simple – a whole chicken and four large bags of chips, no salt, no vinegar – that much Mum and Dad preferred to do themselves.

Kevin and I walked to the chip shop and joined the queue of adults waiting to be served. When our turn came, we placed our order and stood waiting in the tiny shop, relishing the delicious smell of old chip fat as it seeped into our pores. I calculated several times the cost of four chips and one chicken, to be sure that I had enough money with me. When our order was ready, I paid for the meal and reached up for the large brown paper bag and watched as the grease stain on the bottom grew larger before my eyes.

Kevin and I walked a few paces out of the shop with good intentions. Bursting to try a chip – just one – I asked Kevin if he would like one. Always keen to do my bidding, he immediately agreed and poised his hand over the bag as I unfurled the top.

They were hot, fat and greasy. Everything you wanted in a chip.

'You got a bigger one,' I complained to Kevin, so I took another to even the score.

'That's not fair,' he said, as he reached in for a second, feeling around for another big one.

'You did it again!' I said, taking two this time.

That was how it started. Before long we were wolfing them down with abandon, until I stopped to look into the cooling paper bag and realised what we had done. The four thin white paper bags inside the big brown one were all clearly visible now. A few fat chips and all the small burnt shards of potato were all that remained at the bottom of each one. A feeling of dread slid down into the pit of my stomach.

Back at the tent I handed over the bag to Mum, who had six plates lined up on the foldaway table, each one ready to receive a fair share. She easily ripped the soggy bag apart and stared down in disbelief at its meagre contents.

'Is this all you were given?' she snapped.

'Yeah, the bags were quite small,' I said, turning to Kevin for support.

'Did you ask for large?'

'Yeah, hmmm.' I was trying my best to avoid uttering a direct lie.

'Tom,' – Mum beckoned Dad for a second opinion – 'these don't look like large bags.'

Dad stared at what was left of the chips. 'Well I'm going over there to give that gangster a piece of my mind,' he said, getting red in the face, his sense of justice offended. And without hesitation he charged over to the chipper.

He came back several minutes later, redder than ever.

'You two,' he roared at us. 'What were ye playing at? How many chips did ye both eat? You better tell me the truth now or you'll be in more trouble than you are already.'

'A few, Dad,' I whimpered.

'Yeah, just a few, Dad,' copied Kevin.

'Yeah, Dad, they weren't very full when he gave them to us, really.' I was trying to save a hopeless situation.

One good thing about a tent was that parents could not raise their voices to the same extent they did at home. Children's screaming and shouting was acceptable and almost to be expected on a camp site, but parents didn't like to have their parenting overseen or overheard. With this in mind, Dad's voice lowered to a deep, even more threatening growl.

'Off to bed with you now. Not another thing you're getting to eat till tomorrow. Now go!'

We turned to Mum to see where she stood. It was obvious she was completely behind Dad this time.

'Don't ever do anything like that again! That was so greedy! That's a sin, you know!' She too struggled to keep her voice down. 'And to lie about it and make your father go back to the chipper. I don't want to see or hear from either of you till morning.'

There was audible moaning and whingeing from Catherine and Lucy who had returned hungry from their first flirting. On seeing what remained of their dinner, they complained to Mum and Dad that it wasn't fair and pleaded for more chips.

I was exposed and embarrassed in front of my own family, finally found out as a greedy guts – something I'm sure they'd always suspected – and as one who couldn't be left in charge of chips. I felt contrite and remorseful. I wanted to apologise but felt incapable of doing so. Too proud to surrender and lay bare my new self-knowledge for all to examine in the close proximity of the trailer tent, I resolved to say sorry to Mum, privately, in the morning.

Dad frogmarched us to the toilet without saying a word. Then, in the painful brightness of an early evening, Kevin and I lay side by side for several long hours, listening to other children playing and chasing outside, and to my parents and sisters talking in whispers on the other side of the canvas.

Teddy's Whippies

I hated being dragged up and down Dún Laoghaire pier for a walk on Sunday afternoons. I was lazy and there seemed little point to me, walking the length of the promenade and back again. However, this family walk would be transformed if there was a promise of a Teddy's Whippy at the end.

The purchase of six ice-cream cones was an extravagance reserved only for special occasions. Throughout the summer, as the tinkle of the ice cream van that circuited our neighbourhood was heard, we were consistently denied the treat. To halt my whining, Mum told me that the small white and blue van was dirty; she told us of some mysterious neighbourhood child who got seriously ill after eating a cone from the van. When that didn't work, she got cross and told me they were too expensive. All of these reasons were insufficient to dim my desire. But Mum never once gave in. However, the imminent return to school was, for her, the right time to treat us to a Teddy's. It would be the last Teddy's of the year, as the little hatch in the wall would soon close its blue shutters and remain padlocked for the long winter months.

I was terrified of walking on the upper level of the pier. I stayed back from the edge for fear of falling twelve feet, down onto the hard tarmac of the level below. I didn't like the lower level much either, with its twelve-foot drop into the cold lapping waters of the harbour. While Kevin ran on ahead and skirted the edges in daredevil fashion, with Mum and Dad shouting at him to get back, I walked along the flat pier, hugging the wall and holding Mum's hand.

After getting to the lighthouse at the end of the pier, the halfway mark of our walk, we joined the other Sunday strollers, sitting on the blue benches, looking out across the Irish Sea towards England. If the big ferry was arriving or departing, we waved furiously at the tiny figures leaning on the deck rails. I'd wonder if I would ever get a chance for exotic travel to far-off places like England. When we finished looking at the horizon, simultaneously, as if on some unspoken cue, we all stood up and headed back.

The six of us waited patiently in the long queue outside the Teddy's hatch – this was an open window high up in the wall that Dad leaned into and placed our order. If I stood on my tiptoes, I could look through the hatch and see the lady with the white coat and hat, working her ancient-looking piping machine. We waited a long time for our turn to approach the hatch. I was nervous that Dad would lose his patience and call the treat off, but our turn came just as

his sighing reached danger level. The choice on offer was either a plain cone or a 99. We never got 99s. Dad had made his views on that matter quite clear. 'An extra five pence for a small piece of chocolate – bloody robbery!' He ordered six plain cones.

There was no ice cream for us like a Teddy's. Each cone was piped five inches high, with a slightly wilting peak dripping to one side like Elvis's quiff. The ice cream was softer and creamier than any of the numerous blocks we had devoured greedily during the summer months. We wandered slowly and carefully back to our parked car, licking irreverently at our cones and our sticky hands. Somewhere in the back of my mind was a warning from Mum that it was rude to be seen eating and whistling out in public, especially for us girls. But this rule, if it existed at all, was abandoned as each of us, Mum included, indulged, noisily slurping, sucking and making little exclamations of pleasure as we went. We sat back into the car, satisfied, and waited while Dad carefully licked and crunched his way to the bottom of his cone. Then he turned the key in the ignition and we headed for home. I'd have to wait until next summer to get another Teddy's Whippy.

The Winter Menu

My enjoyment of the last two weeks in August was overshadowed by preparations for the return to school. The freedom of the last days of summer was tainted by the arrival in the post of next year's book and uniform list. This meant a trip into Greene's Bookshop and lots of pushing and shoving to try to get my books before stocks ran out. Then another excursion across town with Mum and more queuing in Arnotts to get those disparate pieces of uniform that were not being passed down from Catherine or Lucy this year. This was followed by many hours at the kitchen table covering every single book in brown paper or bumpy leftover wallpaper, to preserve them for the next in line or to ensure a good resale price at the end of the year. Initially I enjoyed cutting out the paper to the right size, making the necessary slits so that it would fold easily at the spine of the book, then folding in the corners and making sure never to get Sellotape on the book itself. The last step was to take my new six-inch ruler from my pink furry pencil case, make three neat lines on the front cover, and carefully write:

Sheila Maher
3rd Class
English

After the fourth book my interest in the task waned, but with Mum watching, there was no getting up from the table until the job was done.

The return to school not only brought that sinking, sick feeling to the pit of my stomach, it also marked a change in the menu at our dinner table. There would be no more strawberries and raspberries for a long time, ice cream would now only make an occasional appearance alongside a slice of warm apple tart. The salad days were over until next summer. School term meant the return of stews, pies, roasts and puddings – not that these were unwelcome, they just seemed less exciting than the foods of summer.

Mum never bored us with the same meal two nights in a row. She tried to keep mealtimes interesting with new recipes she cut out of magazines or scribbled down from some television programme in her Pitman shorthand that only a Second World War code-breaker could decipher.

Sometimes she received new recipes in the post from her more worldly older sister in England. Aunty Mary was privy to new food trends years before us. She was wrapping her chicken breasts in Parma ham, while Mum was still breadcrumbing hers; she was boning and rolling her turkey, while Mum was continuing to stuff the main cavity; she had made tiramisu and banoffee, while we were still being served pavlova.

Even with all of these new recipes at her fingertips, as winter progressed I could usually guess on the way home from school what dinner was likely to be, or at least I'd know the options. As I sat doing my homework at the table Mum buzzed around me, spelling out the occasional word *as Gaeilge* or helping me learn my maths tables. She was an excellent speller and she regularly gave me mini spelling tests as she multitasked our dinner together. For years there had been a certain rhythm to our week's food.

Monday: Stewed or minced meat in some form. This could be a rustic steak and kidney pie or a more fancy 'casserole' laced with some red wine. Rice pudding would always be served for dessert after stew – 'as it's a shame to waste the oven'.

Tuesday: The leftover roast from Sunday would be served today – Monday acted as a buffer to ensure we didn't have to endure the same meat two nights in a row. Sometimes the meat was sliced, covered in leftover gravy, reheated and served with boiled potatoes and fresh vegetables. Or it would be minced for shepherd's pie. Mum had a heavy steel grinder that she screwed onto the side of the table for this sole purpose. She fed chunks of cooked meat into the opening at the top, turned the handle slowly, and I watched with amusement as tiny worms of meat came out of the bottom into her waiting bowl. I was allowed to help with this job; she considered it safe enough – as long as I kept my fingers out of the grinder.

Wednesday: This was a slightly casual day for dinner, with quiche and chips, burger and chips, or maybe fried lamb's liver and chips. Everything was still home-made and prepared freshly that evening, so while the meal may have had the feel of fast-food dining, Mum's workload may have actually been heavier. The deep saucepan of oil that was used to fry our weekly chips sent pungent plumes of smoke up through the entire house that lingered for days. Even my bedroom stank of old chips.

Thursday: Today we'd have pork chops or chicken breasts, served with baked or mashed potato and carrots or marrowfat peas.

Friday: We never had meat on a Friday. Instead, we had scrambled eggs on toast or omelette, or sometimes when Mum was flush, we had fish pie.

Saturday: This was another casual day, with a fry or pasta – when pasta arrived in Ireland – the most likely offering. Spaghetti bolognese, lasagne or moussaka (all considered pasta dishes as far as Mum and Dad were concerned, as they were meals without potato) eventually became Saturday staples.

Sunday: There was always a glorious roast – beef, pork, lamb or chicken – with a special dessert on Sundays. Mum marked the end of the weekend with a culinary high note, which unfortunately signalled the start of another week at school. No sooner did I have the last spoonful of dessert in my mouth than I realised I had only one hour of weekend left.

Within this weekly rota there was always sufficient variety and flexibility for Mum to ensure that the same meals were not served on the same days, week in, week out. And there was always the odd surprise if Mum felt the urge to try one of her new recipes. She never allowed meals to get boring.

Porridge

When schooldays turned winter-cold, I'd pull my uniform off the floor and drag it under the covers, into bed with me. I'd let it warm up a little before wriggling into the polyester shirt and bulky gabardine skirt. With each manoeuvre, blasts of chill bedroom air would waft in under the itchy and heavy blankets. I'd arrive down into the kitchen, dressed in my crumpled uniform, and see my mother's dressing-gown-clad frame leaning over the cooker. She'd be pounding porridge in the thin aluminium double saucepan she kept solely for that purpose. This saucepan was her mother's before her, passed along as though it were a precious family heirloom to ensure hearty breakfasts for successive generations. Mum made porridge the previous night and softened it up in the morning before reheating it.

As the only other early riser, I enjoyed the cosy atmosphere in the kitchen alone with Mum. I stirred the porridge as she went upstairs to help Kevin dress himself and quicken his pace. I heard her knock again on Catherine and Lucy's closed door and gently remind them it was now eight o'clock and time to get up, only to get grunts and growls in reply. Then she returned to the kitchen with Kevin in tow, seated him beside me at the table and served the porridge.

Steam rose from the piping hot bowl she placed in front

of me. With a hand as steady as I could make it, I sprinkled on a heaped spoonful of sugar, being careful to get it all the way out to the edge and over the entire surface of the porridge in an even fashion. I didn't want any large lumps of sugar or any sugarless area. I gently tipped enough cold milk into the bowl to form a thin layer over everything. Then I let it all sit for a few moments.

Mum asked me to run upstairs and waken the girls again. My older sisters orbited around me. I observed them closely, but from a distance. I noticed how they wore their clothes; I knew when Catherine got her first bra; I watched them leave the house to play with friends that lived on streets too far for me to go to alone; I saw them laugh and play pogo stick on the road outside our house, even as it got dark. I wanted to be part of their twosome but I was excluded, so I was jealous and resentful. They never considered me for the role of playmate – as a nine-year-old, I was a baby to them. Their only interaction with me, independent of Mum and Dad, was as occasional baby-sitters, and this rarely worked out well. Their temporary position of authority went to their heads and clashed with my desperation to impress them. When Catherine and Lucy baby-sat for Kevin and me, they denied us our television rights and sent us to bed, early and hysterical.

In trepidation, I knocked on their door and shouted, 'Mum says it's time to get up' – hoping that by blaming this unwelcome interruption on Mum, it would prevent them from shouting back at me. They roared back through the closed door, 'Go away!' 'We know!' 'Leave us alone!' and I returned to my breakfast deflated; they had dented my mood.

My porridge was now cool enough, so I put my spoon deep into the hardening mound. As it pulled away from the side of the bowl it held the bowl's smooth shape. This I felt in my mouth along with its inner bumpy lumpiness. That sweet and milky bowl was hugely soothing and palliative. Warm and comforting, it eased me into the day. I worked my way around the edge of the bowl, scooping out soft ovals of porridge in a steady rhythm, one after the other until the outer rim was gone. The centre I allowed myself to eat in a more haphazard fashion and I took spoonfuls in whatever order I felt like, all the while making sure not to mix it up too much and loose my crunchy sugar topping. Eating porridge was not a simple task of shovelling spoonful after spoonful into your mouth, it required concentration and precision. Cereal could be eaten any old way, each mouthful the same as the next; porridge deserved more respect.

Mum went into the hall and shouted up the stairs one last time. 'Catherine, Lucy, get up *now!*'

The radio was tuned to RTÉ. It crackled and hissed as Mum passed in front of it, going about her preparations. 'Shush,' she said every now and then, as she tried to catch a news headline or a scrap of information amidst my babbling. I stayed quiet for as long as I could and when I deemed enough time had elapsed, I resumed my chat. The stirrings of my sisters and Dad could be heard upstairs – coughing, steps across the landing (I could identify who was up by the weight of their footfall), toilet flushing, the occasional shower.

At twenty minutes to nine I heard pounding on the stairs. Catherine and Lucy burst into the kitchen, both with deep red lines from their pillows scored into their cheeks. Their faces were pale and cross and their short hair stuck up in peaks at the back.

'Aw, not porridge again!' they complained, when they saw Mum preparing to spoon it out for them and they whinged for Corn Flakes or Weetabix instead. With few minutes to spare – as no child of hers was going to be late for school – Mum gave in, something she rarely did. Kevin started to snivel that he was made to eat all his porridge, while they got to eat Corn Flakes. Mum slammed the wooden spoon down on the countertop – a sure sign that her patience had run out – and pounded upstairs to get dressed.

Dad shuffled into the kitchen. Dressed in brown slacks, a co-ordinating sports jacket with mock-leather elbow patches, and shirt and tie, his hair was still damp and the lines made by the teeth of his comb were visible across it. There was the usual choking odour of Old Spice. I found the smell sickening as it mingled with the taste of my porridge and yet it was reassuring and comforting because it was Dad's smell. He prepared his solo Weetabix with some warm milk, ate it in silence and left. Dad was quiet by nature and mornings were definitely too much for him. Generally he talked when he was talked to but he was never one to start a conversation voluntarily. He was one of life's observers, quietly taking it all in from the sidelines and seemingly content to do so.

I lingered around the kitchen for as long as I could – judging the length of time it was going to take me to cycle to my friend Maeve's, ten houses up the road, wait for her, and then cycle to school together. I didn't want to leave the warmth of the kitchen and I fancied the last bit of porridge going cold and hard in the saucepan. Thanks to the preferences of my family I usually got second helpings and the scrape all to myself. I tucked into the last bit straight from the saucepan, and then reluctantly left the house.

I was never happy leaving home for school. I always wanted to stay around my mother all day. I knew this was not a normal feeling for a girl of my age. I was sure none of the other girls in school had such childish desires, so I never articulated them, not even to Maeve. I was at my happiest when I was by my mother's side, helping her and watching as she prepared and cooked our food. I was confident, funny, helpful and loved when I was with Mum in the kitchen. But when I moved beyond our front door, I became unsure of myself, a weak-minded follower and a smart aleck who irritated teachers. School ripped me out of my cosy environment and I hated it for that. Annually I managed to fake a few well-acted 'sick days', so that I could at least lie in bed and listen to the noises of my mother pottering below in the kitchen. From time to time, she'd pop her head into my room to see if I was okay or needed anything. It was hard faking for a whole day, but it was much nicer than being at school.

Eventually the morning arrived when I was the only one in the family eating porridge for breakfast. Mum forgot to make it one Sunday night and the next morning I had to munch my way through a bowl of flimsy Corn Flakes. Then she gave up making it altogether. She said it was a lot of trouble preparing and reheating it just for one. But cold milk poured over thin flakes didn't satisfy me the way porridge had. Even the novelty of watching two Weetabix soak up all the milk in my bowl and turn into a firm brown swamp didn't compensate. I tried warm milk on every cereal we had, but nothing worked. I couldn't re-create the pleasure only porridge could provide, so I gave up trying. School mornings had finally lost their smallest hint of enjoyment for me.

Ham and Cabbage

On my first day back at school I was separated from Maeve. My best friend. The only friend I wanted. She was 'O'Reilly' and I was 'Maher' – 'O' and 'M' – we should not have been separated according to the system that had worked in our favour from our very first day at school. I was miserable sitting in my cold wooden prefab beside strange girls I had never played with before. I was with Brady, Collins, Flynn and Farrell, when I should have been with Murphy, Nolan, O'Donnell and O'Reilly. I'd never had to make a new friend before, I'd always had Maeve. I didn't know how to start all

over with new girls, nor did I want to. I felt completely isolated and excluded.

Not prepared to take it lying down, I spotted my chance when the Principal, Sister Joseph, was on yard duty during break time. I ran to her and in my most polite way asked if I could speak with her.

'Yes,' she said. 'If you can walk with me back to my office. I'm very busy.'

And so I trotted alongside this tall, straight nun as she strode across the school grounds.

'Sister, I want to be moved into 3B,' I said to the side of her flapping veil. 'That's where all the "M"s are, that's where I should be. I don't know why I'm in 3A.' I tried to keep any whine out of my voice. I was talking to the Principal one-to-one, as a girl who knew her own mind.

'There wasn't enough space in 3B this year and so we decided it would be best for you to be in 3A. You can make lots of new friends and you can see Maeve at break time,' she replied, very businesslike.

This was completely unsatisfactory and not going the way I had imagined. I'd been sure there'd been a typing error that had been overlooked, a clerical mistake. I was unaware, until now, that my removal from my usual comfortable group was part of a greater plan.

'We decided that it would be better for both yourself and Maeve to broaden your horizons and make new friends,' Sister Joseph continued, reinforcing her point.

By now she had reached the door to the building that housed the Principal's Office. Her hand was on the handle and she turned to me, her stern look indicating that I was not to follow her inside. This was as far as my grovelling and pleading had got me, to her front door and no further. And when that heavy door thudded in my face, tears filled my eyes. I sloped back to the grey and noisy yard. I'd been singled out for special attention of the wrong kind. The feeling of injustice stung me. This was just not fair.

The whistle was blowing just as I got back to Maeve playing hopscotch. She seemed happy lining up with her new friends to march back to 3B while I resentfully looked at the girls who were to be my classmates until next summer. More tears threatened to choke me as I made my way up the creaky steps of the prefab. I couldn't let Sister Brigid or anyone else see me cry, so I sniffled and swiped surreptitiously at my blotchy face until I felt I must look normal again.

Sister Brigid was a cold beaky nun whose veil prevented even the smallest lock of hair from escaping. While other nuns let a curl or a bang soften their faces a little, Sister Brigid maintained a strict and severe appearance; her veil sat stiffly on the pasty flesh of her face. She kept a brass bell on her desk, which she used as a communication tool. She rang it throughout the day for numerous reasons: to signal the start of a lesson; to signal the end of a lesson; to get our attention if we appeared to drift off; to call for silence when murmuring threatened to drown out her own voice; to indicate that a change of girl was required, as the role of reader moved around the room. Her bell became very annoying during the first few days of school and she continued to use it consistently for the entire year.

I met up with Maeve in the yard after school and we

walked our bicycles home together. I never told her about my failed attempt at pleading with Sister Joseph. Somehow she didn't seem to be as bothered about our separation as I was. I knew it made me look foolish to be begging and crying about the class I was in, while she was just getting on with it, and so I said nothing.

I said goodbye to Maeve at her house and walked home. I didn't tell my mother what had happened, and up to then I'd told her most things. Instead, I sat silently at the kitchen table that afternoon, practising my handwriting on pages that were too closely lined to contain my big round 'a's and long-stemmed 'b's and 'd's. I leaned forward, my nose close to the page, my tongue stuck between my teeth in concentration, and made my way slowly and carefully across each page. I let the noises and smells of home erase the pain of the day, like the shake of an Etch A Sketch, until the next morning.

Three pots were bubbling on the cooker. A pink gristly lump of ham bobbed around in one. In another was cabbage, and the last one held the potatoes. Ham and cabbage. A family favourite. Just what I needed to alleviate my gloom that evening.

When the meal was ready, each of us sat down around our kitchen table to an identical plate. The light was on overhead, the window black from the night sky. A large, moist, pink slice of boiled ham, two small scoops of creamy mash – served with the ice-cream scooper – and an untidy pile of glossy green cabbage shreds. Then we kids got all creative.

Kevin, having been mesmerised by *Close Encounters of the Third Kind*, moved his mashed potato into the centre of his plate and shaped it into a mountain, as Richard Dreyfuss had done in Spielberg's film, with a large crater on top. Into this he piled his cabbage and the slice of ham – his representation of a spaceship with skinny green aliens. Next he poured tomato sauce over the mountain until it oozed down the sides like molten lava. All the while singing the five famous musical notes – 'Doo doo doo doo doo' – in conversation with his alien dinner.

The rest of us indulged him and I especially enjoyed the distraction and light relief of his childish good humour. We gave exaggerated praise to his endeavour, until hunger got the better of him and he devoured it, with Mum getting up and leaning over him to cut up his meat.

Lucy, neat and precise, had made a tiered cake with her dinner. She spread half her mashed potato in a circle on her plate, flattened her cabbage onto this to make the next layer, then placed her slice of ham on top of that and used the remainder of her potato to cream the top of her cake-meal. She then cut into her creation as you would a grand cake and ate her entire dinner, segment by segment.

Catherine, being a teenager, attempted to give us all the impression that she found this play with food a little puerile for her taste, so she cut up her food like an adult. But on her tight, moody face there were traces of envy she could not completely hide.

I attempted to make a swiss roll out of my dinner. I spread potato and cabbage on my slice of ham and then tried to roll it into a log and slice it in cross-sections. Unfortunately it never worked; my swiss roll always unfurled and left me with strips of meat smeared with mash and cold cabbage to eat. I envied Lucy her simple yet effective design but I could never adopt it – that was *her* way of eating ham and cabbage. I would just have to devise another ingenious design, next time we had it for dinner.

Mum ate her dinner in mouthfuls between jump-ups to get tomato sauce, more milk or some salt. Dad just kept his head down and methodically cleared his plate.

The leftover ham found its way into our lunch boxes the next day. Sandwiches made with large slices of white bread, spread with Flora and thin pieces of ham, were cut in half, wrapped in cling film and placed on one side of my lunch box. On the other side sat an apple and a treat. The treat alternated between two Garibaldi biscuits and a Jammie Dodger or, if I was really, really lucky, a home-made chocolate toffee square or a stick of Twix. All of this was washed down with some tepid milk straight from one of the hundreds of cartons that had been sitting in the school yard all morning.

Leftover mash was saved for Friday's tea and became potato cakes – flattened triangles of mashed potato mixed with a little flour, fried in butter, sliced open and served with melting butter on each half – scrambled eggs on the side.

Leftover cabbage was not quite so popular. Mum never wanted to throw any food away and so she put it in the fridge. The following evening she reheated it on a plate over a saucepan of boiling water, and it sat on the table going cold again, as we avoided it in favour of the fresh alternative. Eventually, and to set an example to us children, Mum or Dad felt morally obliged to eat it, so that it wouldn't 'go to waste', as 'that'd be a sin'.

Apples

We were not poor. We had a nice home. I had a bedroom that I only had to share with Kevin, though it was always cold as the heating was not used upstairs, except during sub-zero temperatures and even then we had to ask permission to turn it on. We had warm clothes to wear (albeit a mixture of home-made and many hand-me-down ensembles); we went on holidays (in a tent or borrowed caravan). We were not deprived. But I was keenly aware that Mum and Dad always watched every penny they spent. So from time to time they announced a new scheme they had devised, an idea to save money, or at least make it spread a bit further.

One such scheme had been to get a friend of theirs, who had a knitting machine, to custom-knit our school jumpers. For several weeks, Ethnea busied herself in her spare bedroom, sliding bobbins of navy wool this way and that across the many tiny, darting needles of her machine. Every few days the phone rang, and while Ethnea waited on the other end of the line, Mum grabbed her inch tape and pulled it along the length of our arms, or down our backs from neck to bum, or around our waists, and then relayed the measurements to Ethnea, who presumably inputted our vital statistics into her magic machine.

Mum was thrilled when the three navy jumpers arrived

and each one fitted perfectly. However, the nuns at school were not at all happy to see the three Maher sisters lining up in the assembly hall and the school yard in a non-regulation shade of blue. It was not going to be tolerated. No such precedent could be set or everyone would be at it. And so it was back to Arnotts we were marched. A small fortune was handed over for three jumpers of the correct hue. Mum was now out of pocket for wool, a thank-you gift for Ethnea and the cost of three new shop-bought jumpers. At least all was good with the nuns again.

This year Mum and Dad settled, somewhat arbitrarily, on apples as a potential source of savings. The first money-saving scheme involved an autumn afternoon in an orchard. This was to be a productive activity; not only was there fresh air and exercise to be had, but as suburban kids, we were getting a rare opportunity to connect with nature and help our parents into the bargain. Kevin and I were too short to be of much assistance with the apple-picking. Our job was to gather as many as possible off the ground, but that meant Dad had to be put on quality control to check each apple for worms and rot. Then we were given the task of pointing out apples to the taller members of the family. I saw through this ploy. It was a made-up job to keep us quiet, and it was boring. I busied myself with eating instead. I ate a lot of apples, more than I thought anyone could possibly eat in one afternoon, and I groaned with cramps all the way home.

When all the orchard apples we had harvested were eaten, Mum and Dad tried their next scheme. They got up very early one Saturday morning, leaving Catherine to supervise us from her bed, and drove into the Smithfield Markets.

Mixing with the traders and shopkeepers who were rushing about negotiating deals and discounts, they bought boxes of apples and oranges at wholesale price. They didn't enter into any bargaining, but they came home delighted with the savings they had made all the same. The boxes were left in the garage and we were told to help ourselves.

Our lunch boxes were not complete without at least one small apple, now damp and smelling of egg sandwich, in the corner. Any request for a snack, or a whine of 'I'm hu-ungry', was met with 'Have an apple'. Though soon Mum realised that the more fruit was in the house, the more we ate. Add to this the rapid rotting that occurred in the bottom of the boxes, the free bags of apples Mum gave away to friends and family, the early trips to the market, and the huge numbers of crumbles and tarts she had to make in order to consume the apples before the rotting set in, and this scheme did not in the end seem like such a great idea.

Apple tart, apple purée, apple crumble, apple charlotte, apple fritters, apple amber, apple betty, apple with Madeira cake on top, sponge with apple stuck in it, apple and blackberry crumble, baked apples, apple sauce with pork, apples for school lunches, apples for snacks. Apples until they were coming out of our ears. I couldn't wait until they were all gone. I played my part by eating several a day – even if I wasn't hungry, when I passed a bowl of them, I took one. I was relieved to see the bottom of each box. I don't think I was alone, for quietly the idea was dropped and the trips to Smithfield thankfully ended.

Moondust in the Phoenix Park

Mum stood by my bed, gently nudging me from my sleep and telling me to get up. It was dark outside and I wanted to roll over and block out this unwelcome interference. We had to get ready quickly, she said, and catch the bus. Then I remembered what day it was, what was happening. The Pope was coming to Dublin. I jumped out of bed and put on the clothes that were laid out for me. I gobbled my breakfast, with not only Kevin at the table beside me but Catherine and Lucy as well. Dad had a cold and was staying in bed for the day.

It was exciting to be awake in the middle of the night. I carried a flask and a lunch box in a small plastic bag. Mum was loaded down with the big bag we took to the beach and a few foldaway stools. We made our way slowly to the main road, and as we walked, more and more people shut their front doors behind them and joined the procession, all heading in the one direction. There was a queue for the bus by the time we got to the stop. We joined it and stood shivering until two headlights appeared out of the darkness and pulled up beside us. We squeezed on the bus and I tried to sleep on my feet as I stood swaying all the way to the

outskirts of the Phoenix Park, in a part of the city that was unfamiliar and intimidating to me.

We ate most of our food in enclosure Yellow 15 before Mass started, and I was hungry the rest of that long day. The initial excitement eventually gave way to boredom as we stood about waiting for the Pope to arrive.

Then a girl in the enclosure beside us said, 'Wanna try some?' In her outstretched hand she held a small colourful foil packet.

'Yeah,' I replied, unsure of what I was signing up for but I was bored and hungry. Into my palm she spilled a mound of irregular-shaped shards of candy.

'You do this,' she said, and she whacked a fistful into her mouth.

Without hesitation, I copied her.

Nothing could have prepared me for the experience I was about to have. My mouth was tingling and sore and I felt like choking all at the same time. I was stunned. I was confused. I was giddy. This was the most frightening and exciting sweet I had ever tasted. I asked my neighbour to let me see the packet again, and I looked at it closely.

'It's Moondust,' she said, and she turned on her heel, back to her allotted space.

The Popemobile passed by close to our enclosure. I cheered and clapped and stuck my Instamatic camera in the air over my head to get a photograph. Then he was gone and I thought of the long walk to the bus stop, the queuing and pushing to get on, the lurching bus journey back to our road and then the walk to our house. I was tired and wanted to be home already.

Grandma's Scones

Our Sunday morning ritual was cast in stone. After eleven o'clock Mass, we visited Grandma, along with Mum's brother and his family. One of Mum's brothers had died a few years earlier, but his wife kept up the visits and she and her family also joined the weekly crush in Grandma's modest kitchen.

Grandma was a widow and she lived alone. She went to Mass every morning of her life, sat in the same pew and chatted to neighbours afterwards. Then she shuffled down to Ranelagh village or, if she was tired, she only went as far as her local grocer, Morton's, to get what she needed for her dinner. The rest of the morning she spent reading the newspaper, listening to Gay Byrne on the radio and preparing a full three-course meal for herself, which she ate at midday. Some afternoons she gardened, or she baked sponges and tarts for herself or those neighbours she referred to as 'elderly', though usually they were many years her junior. Some afternoons she dozed in her armchair in the sitting room, where we'd find her when we called on a surprise visit.

Grandma was the ideal and rare species of granny, and I was aware of this from a very young age. She never gave out to me or interfered; she didn't criticise; she was a martyr who never complained. Even when oozing leg ulcers throbbed or large cuts were slow to heal on her thin-skinned hands, making her life more difficult, she just shrugged and carried on regardless. She was funny and most of all she laughed at herself. I only had one grandparent and I knew I got quality not quantity.

Maeve, on the other hand, grumbled about her granny when she visited. She had too many complaints and minor illnesses for Maeve's liking. When I called for Maeve to play, Mrs Sheehy often obliged us to play 25s with her. I loved playing cards, and as I only ever got to play them on summer holidays in our tent or at Christmas-time, I was always keen to sit down and play a hand with Mrs Sheehy. But Maeve had other plans and she'd drag me away to play in her Wendy House in the back garden instead.

I found it hard to empathise or sympathise with Maeve and other girls in school who gave out about interfering and grumpy grannies, so I kept quiet and kept Grandma to myself.

Although we usually saw Grandma during the week, I never minded a second visit. Sunday morning was special, with all the family in the kitchen talking and laughing, and we got to play with our cousins. In preparation for our arrival, Grandma baked scones. When Mum opened the front door, the smell of warm, damp dough drifted up to greet us, along with Grandma's 'Hell-o-oh', from down in the kitchen.

The kitchen chairs were occupied according to seniority and gender, the ladies of the family took the few seats at the table, the men and children sat on footstools, garden chairs and deck chairs or leaned against the dresser, loaded with crockery and glassware, or any clear wall space we could find. In the middle of the room, under the window, was the table, and in the centre of the table was a wire rack, on which a dozen golden scones were cooling. A butter dish and a selection of jams, usually home-made, sat beside a stack of delicate plates, small fluted cups and a bundle of Grandma's butter knives with their strange round tips and square ivory handles. She hadn't moved with the times to cutlery with green plastic handles like ours.

As soon as the initial greetings and polite chit-chat were over, someone – usually one of the big boy cousins – would lean in and get busy buttering a scone, or maybe even two. That would trigger the stampede. There was no time to lose if you wanted to be guaranteed your share, yet it was difficult to find a gap in the mêlée around the table.

Grandma's younger sister, my Grandaunt Maudie, got the bus out to Ranelagh and sat at the kitchen table on fifty-one Sundays of the year – the only exception was when she was away on her annual trip to Lourdes. While Grandma was all hugs and flour-covered housecoats, Maudie was stylishly dressed in tailored skirt suits, cinched at the waist with a narrow belt to accentuate its smallness, deep tan tights and very high heels. When she wasn't smoking, either a barbed comment or a hacking cough came out of her mouth.

I was wary of Maudie. But I was told to be nice to her, as she was 'poor oul' Maudie'. Mum said she had had a hard life. After marrying late, she had only a decade of childless marriage before her husband suddenly dropped dead of a heart attack. At fifty, Maudie was alone with no home and no source of income. The Christian Brothers of Synge Street let her live in a building they owned on Grantham Street for a nominal rent.

She, in turn, took in the occasional tenant as a source of income. It was a life-saving arrangement that gave her a roof over her head and supplemented her meagre widow's pension. For most of the year, Maudie's life was confined to the areas around Camden Street, trips across town to Clery's, and Sundays at her sister's in Ranelagh. She rarely went further afield, except for Lourdes, that is, which seemed pretty exotic to me. For all of this, I was supposed to view Maudie in a softer, kinder light. But I couldn't, it only made it clear to me why she was so hard. I wasn't the only one who found her difficult company. Dad had long struggled to be nice to her. One of her catch phrases was 'Well, that's country people for ye! Present company excepted' – with a brief nod in Dad's direction. This made him, a proud Tipperary man, quietly seethe.

So one Sunday it was with some trepidation, when I spotted a momentary gap in the scrimmage, that I approached the table where Maudie sat near the few remaining scones. I hoped I hadn't caught her attention. As she regarded herself as a style icon, my appearance had come in for criticism before. 'That skirt's very long, isn't it?' 'What did you do to your hair?' 'I see you bite your nails. Terrible habit, especially for a girl.'

But that day she delivered the cruellest comment of them all. As I moved towards the table I entered her field of vision and out it rasped: 'You're a fine big girl.'

With my arm already outstretched for the longed-for scone, I didn't want to retract it and let her see how much she had upset me. Even though my anticipated pleasure had just evaporated in her toxic ether, I picked a scone and buttered it. I placed it on a small plate and looked down at butter melting into each half as I walked across the kitchen, back to my spot against the wall. Had everyone noticed? It seemed like the entire room drew breath. My mother definitely had. Deflated and angry, I sank my teeth into the scone, wanting the comfort of it, yet not wanting it at the same time. I said little for the rest of the morning and watched, head bowed, as the rest of my family continued to eat, drink cups of tea and chat.

Grandma, wanting to salve my wounded pride, shuffled over to her dresser, and from behind the legs of several of her guests, she removed her biscuit tin. A battered short-bread tin, its original contents had been devoured decades ago. She refilled it regularly with her own selection of biscuits. Some weeks there were only Rich Tea, Marietta and Malted Milk. On a more fruitful foray into the tin, I might find a Telex, a Breakaway and a few Jacob's Club Milks. You never knew what kind of selection you were going to get. When Grandma asked if you would like a biscuit, it was always better to wait until the lid was off before answering.

As Grandma presented the tin to me that morning, I felt all eyes on me. Ignoring etiquette, throwing aside the manners she had upheld and passed on for almost eighty years, she bypassed Maudie and her daughters-in-law and opened the tin before me. On any other Sunday I would have been thrilled to have had the pick of the tin before my big cousins got stuck in, but that day I felt confused. I wanted to take the Orange Club Milk but thirteen pairs of eyes were watching me. And so with cheeks burnt red with embarrassment, and even though I knew I was disappointing Grandma, I said thank you, but no. I was full.

Irish Stew

I assumed the ability to make a delicious Irish stew would be in my mother's DNA, along with her pale green eyes, curly, wiry hair, and her tendency to turn bright red after only a few minutes in mild June sunshine. But I was mistaken. Even though Mum cowered in the face of Irish stew, she felt it her duty to serve it regularly – it being one of the few traditional Irish dishes in her repertoire.

There were several reasons why Mum cringed when serving Irish stew. Firstly, to her it looked like poor people's food. The thin, watery liquid that glistened under the bright fluorescent kitchen light; the grey pieces of fatty lamb floating around in it; and only overcooked carrots and soggy potato as an accompaniment – all tended to support this view.

Secondly, she thought she was no good at making it – this was not something Mum regularly admitted. She believed she was doing something wrong. Should the gravy be so thin and runny? She experimented, using barley as well as potato to thicken it. What about the greasy scum on top? Hoping no one was looking, she'd turn her back to us and try to skim the fat off before dishing it out. Were there enough potatoes in the stew? She cooked extra, only to be left with a huge bowl of spuds at the end of the meal.

There were too many uncertainties for Mum when it came to Irish stew. She was not confident about it at all, and when she did serve it, she brought it to the table with an apologetic air. She never fished for compliments on these days. 'Well …? What has anyone got to say?' was her usual casual question when she knew she had done a damn good job and deserved some praise. And we'd all mumble, through full mouths, 'Mmmm, it's gorgeous, Mum.' 'Yeah! Lovely, thanks.' But on Irish stew days, she kept quiet, there were no prompts as she served the meal.

It's true to say that Mum was right – her stew didn't look good. It swished around on our plates, leaving an oily slick at the edges, which turned into solid white fat when it cooled. It looked insipid and sad. But if you closed your eyes – well, that was a different story. It tasted delicious. The moist tenderness and unique earthy taste of lamb, with a strong kick of thyme, made it worth enduring the slop. It may have left a film of fat on the roof of your mouth and on your lips, but with a wipe of the back of your hand and the sleeve of your school jumper, that was soon gone, while the wonderful flavours of the Irish stew lingered on.

Monkey Nuts

On our last day at school before the Hallowe'en midterm holiday, Sister Brigid was sick. This added to my excitement at getting a break from school. Mrs Piggott from 3B marched across the yard and into our prefab at ten past nine, and without saying a word, wrote on the blackboard the exercises we were to do for the morning. She departed with a stern warning to us to be quiet – *Ciúnas*! A girl from sixth class, with neat, long, blond hair and socks pulled up to her knees, sat at Sister Brigid's desk. She watched us and made sure we stayed quiet and did our work.

After break time, Mrs Piggott came back to our classroom and told us to follow her, we were going to join her class for the rest of the morning. I was thrilled. We were going to the new building and into Maeve's classroom; we could be classmates for one morning.

We trotted in pairs across the yard and filed into the bright warm environs of 3B. I waved over at Maeve when we entered. She smiled and waved back. I wondered how we were all going to fit. Mrs Piggott told us we wouldn't need chairs for now, as we were going to stand around the room and have an Irish spelling test. A test without warning seemed a bit unfair; an Irish spelling test on the day before our midterm break was just plain sneaky. We were trapped.

All fifty-six girls lined up tightly around the walls of the room, encircling Mrs Piggott, who leaned her bum against a table in the centre. Slowly she made her way around the room, calling out words – *leabhar … bríste … fuinneog …* If a spelling was incorrect, the shamed girl sat down in the centre of the room; only the good spellers remained standing. It was agonising waiting for my moment under pressure, under scrutiny.

'Síle Ní Meachair – *cathaoir,*' she said, when my turn came.

'*C-A-T-H-A-O-I-R.*' I spelled it out slowly and clearly.

'No. Sit down,' she said.

Surprise registered on my face – I was sure I'd spelled it correctly – but conceding to her greater knowledge, I moved to sit down in an empty chair. But I was too late for the keen eye of Mrs Piggott. My surprise had registered with her too and had been mistaken for defiance or incredulity or some other unacceptable form of pupil behaviour.

'*Anseo,* Síle!' she ordered sharply, pointing to the ground in front of her, where I was to stand. She was still leaning against the table and her arms were folded tightly across her chest. 'What was that face for?' she demanded. 'Do you think you know better than me?'

'No, Mrs Piggott.'

'Do you think I'm wrong and you are right? Is that it?'

'No, Mrs Piggott.'

'Do you know what "humble" means, Miss Maher? Do you know this song, Miss Maher?' She began to taunt me with a rendition of a bad song that was familiar to me.

Oh Lord it's hard to be humble
When you're perfect in ev-ver-y wa-ay
I can't wait to look in the mirror
'Cause I get better lookin' each day …

On and on she sang. Into my face she shouted the entire song, as I stood there belittled and red in front of my class and girls who weren't that familiar to me. Relentless, she was breathless and red in the face too, but she was enjoying herself.

'Now sit down and don't let me see you doing that again,' she bellowed at me.

I sat down, miserable and confused, wondering why my facial expression had provoked such an extreme reaction. I bowed my head and tried to hide my tears but my short hair made that impossible. My nose was dribbling and I needed a tissue.

The bell rang at ten to one, before the test was over. A few brainy girls were still standing, undefeated by her spelling challenges. I left her classroom as quickly and as discreetly as I could. I didn't look back or wait for Maeve.

I now had a week to forget about Mrs Piggott and my miserable school life.

Our Hallowe'en costumes were far from elaborate. Mostly they consisted of a couple of Dad's old sports jackets, with the sleeves rolled up, and masks with funny faces. I found the biggest plastic bag I could carry and Kevin and I went outside to meet up with Maeve, and her sister and brother. Together we barged from door to door, collecting treats. We crowded around front doors and held open our bags for whatever goodies the lady of the house was dispensing. 'Something for the Hallowe'en party?' was our call. It was hard to tell what was being deposited in our bags, as adult hands concealed their contents. Although frequently asked, we never performed songs or dances. There were a few houses where the owners turned off all lights to the front, pretending no one was at home; a few more where we knew children were not welcome; and others where we were downright afraid to knock on the door. We stayed out in the darkness until most houses in the neighbourhood were accounted for. Then we said goodbye to each other and ran indoors, eager to examine our haul.

Kevin and I spilled the contents of our bags onto the kitchen table. Sadly our booty was never that exciting. There was only one small bar of chocolate, a lollipop or two, and a few old sticky penny sweets with paper so tightly wrapped around and imbedded in them that I ended up eating most of the paper as well. The bottom of my bag had been weighed down, but mostly with monkey nuts and apples, which covered the table. It was clear now that the hands that had mysteriously filled our bags in the semi-darkness had almost all been full of nuts.

Ignoring Mum and Dad's remonstrations about not making ourselves sick, Kevin and I ate as much of our haul as we could, starting with the nice stuff. Then I methodically munched my way through a significant portion of nuts. Knowing Mum was partial to them, I filled a bowl for her.

Later, Kevin and I moved into the sitting room for games with Mum and Dad. While Catherine and Lucy claimed they were no longer willing to participate in such childish games, they hovered around the room as the rest of us got our faces wet and messy. A gentle prodding from Mum almost got them taking a turn but something held them back. They nibbled at some nuts and watched instead. I wasn't able to get a bite out of the apples bobbing in the basin of water, but it was fun watching Mum and Dad try. It was equally hopeless trying to get a mouthful of the apple dangling in the open doorway, until Dad held the string for me. These games flagged quickly and then it was time for Kevin and me to go to bed. Aware that an entire week of freedom stretched ahead of us, we didn't complain.

Meat Loaf

Meat loaf was end-of-the-month food. When the freezer was empty and there was nothing left to magic into a tasty meal, it was time to serve up this less than popular dish. In order to trick us into believing that we weren't just eating a block of minced meat, Mum found a recipe that camouflaged it well. This involved a glaze of brown sugar, tomato purée, Worcestershire sauce and mustard – four powerfully pungent flavours mixed together and spread on top of the meat towards the end of its cooking. The sweet smell of the sugar and tomato permeated the kitchen instantly.

Getting the meat loaf out of its tin was a tricky operation. Mum needed two fish slices – one at each end. I held the loaf tin with a tea towel while Mum lifted the bending, wobbling block of grey-brown meat gingerly onto a heated carving plate, her dexterity saving it from the floor each time. She cut the meat loaf with the carving knife as part of the pretence that we were eating something more special than minced meat, the fatty bits of the animal, the bits you don't want to think about or are too embarrassed to mention. And she cut the slices an inch thick. The fact that Mum was carving at all, however, was in itself a giveaway, as carving was Dad's job. Grease oozed from the loaf as it was cut. I looked around at the faces of my siblings. Lucy's curled lip and Catherine's look of horror were, if noticed by Mum, ignored. In trepidation we picked up our knives and forks and got stuck in.

Our slices of glistening meat with the sharp sugary topping came with peas and mashed potato. I winced at the first mouthful, but the sweetness and eye-watering sting of the glaze somehow combined well with the greasiness of the meat and they cancelled each other out. What I got was a grainy, onion-and-meaty mouthful – not half as distasteful as anticipated. However, the large amount left on my plate, the fat hardening to a white solid, said all there needed to be said about meat loaf.

Dad, regularly and jokingly referred to as the human rubbish bin, always cleared his plate. He also tended to eat any remaining vegetables or potatoes that may have otherwise gone to waste at the end of a meal. He had a big appetite for plain and simple food. So I was surprised to see him leaving some meat loaf and mashed potato on his plate as well. It was definitely time to refill the freezer.

The large chest freezer lived in our garage. When the lid was lifted, a cold steam seeped out, like the dry ice on *The Top of the Pops* stage. The baskets on top were regularly replenished with sliced pans, home-made scones, sausages, frozen peas, bags of breadcrumbs and dinner leftovers stored in old Flora cartons. Underneath these baskets was the main reason we had a freezer. There, in the coldest part, lay all of our meat. A different shape, size or shade of red indicated to Mum's experienced eye which cut of which animal she was looking at. When the silver floor of the freezer was visible – which it now was – it was time to contact Tom Hickey, the butcher. Mum and Dad usually discussed what they wanted before Mum phoned – this was a big biannual financial outlay, so she wanted his assistance with the decision-making.

When the order was ready, she specified clearly to Mr Hickey how she wanted the hind quarter to be prepared and bagged; the T-bones separated from the sirloin; the mince divided into two-pound bags; how all the roasts and round steak were to be presented.

A few days later I went with Mum to collect her order. The counter boys marched in file out to our car carrying open cardboard boxes, laden with individual bags of bloody meat. Rapidly they identified each item to Mum. They had a numbering system, too, in case she needed it: in bright blue marker each bag was numbered, each number corresponding to a little piece of the cow in a picture on the shop wall. It seemed very complicated to me.

Dad was on standby when we got home – there was not a second to be wasted, no meat was given the chance to go off. Working swiftly together, like a relay team, they filled the base of the freezer, Mum making a mental note of what went where. Then she turned the dial up fully and blasted the meat with cold air.

Mum didn't put the butcher's burgers to freeze right away, she kept them aside. While the rest of the meat was chilling, Dad painstakingly took one burger at a time and reshaped it into two new burger patties of a modest size. This was his idea. 'Quarter Pounders' might be the norm in America or in Dublin chip shops, but he considered them unnecessarily large and wasteful. So Mum respected his minor role in matters culinary and in the space of an hour he doubled the number of burgers we got from the butcher; then she placed them in the freezer.

In late summer, when lamb was a little cheaper than in spring, the procedure would be repeated. Gigot chops, loin chops, cutlets, legs, shoulders – an entire lamb joined what was left of the cow in the depths of our freezer. Year in, year out, cut by carnivorous cut, we chewed our way through animal after animal.

A Finger in My Mash

Mealtimes were not always fun; six of us squashed around the square table, cheek by jowl, shoulders and arms touching, looking closely at each other, listening to each other chewing loudly, or someone gulping and swallowing their milk noisily. I'd shiver when the tine of a fork scraped at an angle across a plate. Seven days a week, fifty-two weeks a year – this was not enjoyable.

My 'end of the table' was the troublesome one. Dad and I sat opposite each other with Catherine at right angles between us; three quick-tongued and hot-tempered individuals in such close proximity that our dinner plates touched. At this time Catherine was well into her stride as a teenager, full of sulks and causing tension. I resented how she could change the temperature of a room just by entering it. She had kind moments when she let me try on her jewellery or let Lucy borrow her clothes but these were the exception; sulking and scowling was her norm. I, on the other hand, was opinionated and vocal. My school reports were already peppered with complaints such as 'disruptive', 'troublesome', 'talks back when corrected'. We were three strong personalities confined in a tight space, dinner in and dinner out.

Dad, who had been known to swing from quiet and uncommunicative to loud roaring in a matter of seconds, had become increasingly unpredictable. At some meals he seemed withdrawn and vacant, and let arguments take place around him and wash over him. At other times he was easily angered and flared up quickly. I noticed that an air of tension had crept into the kitchen at dinner time in the last few weeks; no one knew when, or if, his temper would flare and at whom it would be directed.

Down the other end of the table were Mum, Lucy and Kevin. They watched quietly, out of boredom, shock or wisdom – I never knew which – while our end of the table combusted one evening. Dad shouted louder and louder; Catherine screeched hysterically; I roared deliberately-made-to-inflame comments at each of them, until it all became too much for Mum.

'Stop it! Stop it the lot of you!' she shouted in a tremulous voice – it was never difficult to provoke Mum to tears. 'I'm fed up with you all. I've been working all day to get this dinner ready and you've just ruined it.'

She left the table and stood over the sink, blowing her nose and patting her eyes. I stared down at my half-eaten dinner. I knew I couldn't leave the table, that would divert too much of the tension in the room onto me. I'd have to stay and see if I could redeem myself. But if there was going to be trouble, I wasn't going to suffer alone. And so I started the blame game.

'It's all your fault. Happy now?' I muttered out the side of my mouth to Catherine. I was half hoping Mum would hear me, chime in and blame her too. But she didn't.

Catherine's frustration at not having won the initial argument and now having to deal with a tearful mother and upstart young sister got the better of her. Right under my nose she launched an attack on my dinner.

'So there!' she snarled, a big greasy index finger diving into my hill of mashed potato. When she pulled out her finger, it left behind a clean tunnel, boring deep into my mash.

Even though she did this kind of thing regularly, it always left me speechless. There was no lower blow I could imagine. The disrespect, the utter disregard for precious food, stunned me into silence. I assessed her plate. I could swipe all her peas onto the floor. I could pick up her pork chop and fling it against the kitchen wall. I could slam my fist into her potato. These images flashed before my eyes but I couldn't bring myself to execute any one of them. To waste and destroy food in such a manner was anathema to me. Instead, I appealed, in my best whine, to my seething Dad and snivelling Mum to sort Catherine out; to deliver the appropriate punishment.

Sometimes Mum would sit down and try to break the ice, and a timid conversation might follow until it was time to vacate the kitchen. Other times we carried on in a strained, chewing silence for the rest of the meal, until each of us had cleaned our plates. We'd mutter our excuses and leave Mum in the kitchen, alone.

That evening I felt a strong sense of guilt as I looked at my red-eyed mother. I saw that my behaviour was not making her life any easier. So I said quietly, 'Sorry, Mum', and got a faint thank-you smile and a weak pat between my shoulder blades.

Peas

Lucy was generally considered to be 'the good one' in our family, the child who caused little or no trouble. Catherine was too moody to be a contender for the title, I was too hot-tempered, and Kevin, he was just Kevin, the baby. So out of us lot, like cream, Lucy rose to the top as the best-behaved child and she was rarely at the receiving end of Dad's temper.

The smallest of the three girls, Lucy had had an operation for a squint when she was little. She had feet that turned in, too, and had to wear her shoes on the wrong feet to correct them. The rest of us decided that, for all of these reasons, Dad felt she needed extra protection.

He wasn't so patient with the rest of us. I'd seen him take after Kevin when he'd been naughty. He'd chase him round and round the two apple trees in the back garden, sports jacket open and flapping wildly, coins and keys jangling loudly in his trouser pockets. He'd curse Kevin under his breath and call for him to 'Come here, ye little brat' until he pounced on him and landed a loud whack on his bottom.

Several times he'd thundered up the stairs in pursuit of me, as I locked myself into the toilet to escape a slap, knowing my attempt at avoidance was futile – I had to come out eventually. (This strategy had been known to commute my sentence. Dad's slaps were less enthusiastic after half an hour of cooling off time. However, it was a strategy that required much resolve to stay put inside that tiny, locked cubicle. I also had to pray that no one else needed to use the solitary toilet or else I was at Dad's mercy.) When I did come out, I was sent to my room for the rest of the evening.

As for Catherine, Dad sat within arm's reach of her at the dinner table, so she learned to be deft at jumping out of her seat to avoid a swipe.

Lucy's veil of protection, however, did not save her one evening when Mum served peas with our dinner. Lucy didn't like peas. She spent the entire meal moving them around her plate, hiding some under a piece of discarded fat or sinew, accidentally-on-purpose knocking a few onto the table or floor. Furtively she looked at Dad as she executed each of these ingenious plans to get rid of her peas. Without looking in her direction, Dad was keenly aware of her agenda.

I carefully fingered my last few peas onto my fork and brought them to my mouth, and put my knife and fork together on my plate as I was told to do, a signal that I was ready for my next course.

Lucy nervously twitched her cutlery, trying in vain to hide a few peas under her knife and fork.

'Eat your peas, Lucy,' Dad suddenly snapped across the table.

'I'm not hungry any more,' Lucy tried.

'They're good for you, now eat them.' Dad's voice got louder.

'I don't like peas,' Lucy snivelled.

'Everyone else can eat them and so will you.' Dad's face turned red, a hue that signalled impending danger.

Lucy bent her head low and started to cry. The rest of us watched in silence. And then she was gone. She bolted out of her chair and made a brave dash for the door. Dad jumped up out of his seat and tried to intercept her but he was slower than usual and having to manoeuvre around Catherine's chair hindered his progress. He was not quick on his feet and certainly no match for a twelve-year-old. So he let her run upstairs and went into the hall and bellowed up after her, 'That's it, Lucy. No dessert for you. And I don't want to see you down here for the rest of the evening, ye hear!'

He returned to the kitchen, slammed the door and rejoined us at the table. His breathing was laboured from the sudden exertion and he gripped the edge of the table, shaking from pent-up anger, his forehead glistening like a skinless chicken breast.

Lucy's crown as 'the good one' certainly slipped a little that night.

Grace After Meals

I couldn't put my finger on it. The atmosphere in the house was different. It wasn't just that the house was quiet most of the time, it was because Mum was quiet. She still gave orders and told me what to do, but when she wasn't doing that, she was quiet. She didn't sing to herself. She didn't turn the radio on every time she entered the kitchen. I'd find her staring out the kitchen window at our back garden, or at her own reflection if it was dark outside. She was still.

Foolishly I mentioned a new prayer to her. I was doing my best to help lift the fug that had settled over our house. I was seeking approval. I yearned too desperately to be her favourite. Mum and Dad didn't have favourites, but that didn't prevent me, in the heat of a row, from taunting them with accusations that another sibling was their favourite. Dad brushed off such accusations angrily as 'bloody rubbish'. Mum usually turned misty-eyed and bestowed a hug of guilt on her accuser. I wanted some sign that I was her pet. But no treat or extra time together was ever enough. I wanted her to come right out and say it to my face, which she never did. So I resorted to obsequious strategies from time to time.

On this occasion, I told her about the prayer we read in my religion book in school – it was 'Grace After Meals'. Not only could you start a meal with a prayer, but you could end it with one too. I thought it would cheer her up if she could see that she had one 'holy' child. I knew how important religion was to her and I hoped to use it to wipe away that air of sadness that hung over her like a shroud. And it worked. She thought it was a great idea. 'You can't do a good thing too often,' she said, smiling benevolently at her youngest daughter.

The next day I regretted planting that seed. As we scraped the last bits of stew from our plates, Mum took out my religion book and started to recite the new prayer we were all to say. Catherine and Lucy groaned loudly and gave me dirty looks. Mum persisted. For several days she insisted on chanting the prayer – as we made moves to leave the table.

'We have a lot to pray for,' she snapped, glaring at each one of us in turn.

I didn't understand her subtle allusions, but I obediently sat down again to pray with her.

Mum found it hard to judge the best time to say this prayer. In our house the unspoken and vague rule about leaving the dinner table was that in order to leave, your plate or bowl had to be clean and everyone else had to be nearly finished too, only then could you ask to be excused. Permission might be granted and it might not – leaving the table was at Mum's discretion. If she had something to say or felt the meal had been too rushed, she might refuse permission and we were all required to sit at the table until she decided we had spent sufficient time together as a family. So picking the right time to say a final prayer was a dilemma. Saying it while some of us were still eating was rude and rushed us to the end of our meal. Waiting until the last person had finished meant there were only two or three people left at the table, so she ended up saying the prayer by herself or with one unfortunate chorister. This last approach encouraged Kevin and I to gobble the remainder of our food and jump down from the table together, so that neither of us had to suffer the embarrassing intimacy of saying a prayer, alone, out loud, with Mum.

Thankfully Mum knew when she was beaten. She didn't try too hard to impose the 'Grace After Meals'. Instead, she insisted each of us bless ourselves upon leaving the table. A lasting compromise we were all grateful for.

Banana and Jam Sandwiches

The winter had set in and it was dark as I walked home from school with Maeve. Our gabardine coats couldn't keep out the chill and my bare legs turned purple with the cold, but still we walked slowly, pushing our bicycles, chatting all the way. We were later than usual, as we had Irish dancing after school, but there was still time to get our homework done before dinner. I said goodbye to Maeve at her house and sauntered the rest of the way home.

I arrived at our front gate to witness Mum and Dad getting out of the car ahead of me. From the bottom of the driveway, in the evening gloom, I watched them unnoticed. I saw Mum help Dad out of the car and link him up the steps to the front door. He looked smaller, stooping, no longer the tall handsome man I saw in my baby photos. He looked frail as he shuffled into the house.

I didn't say a word when Mum placed a banana and jam sandwich in front of me for dinner. I lost myself in the novelty of eating fruit between two slices of bread. The banana had started to dissolve and it was soft and runny, delicious and sweet.

Something told me it would be nice to help Mum clean up

after our tea that evening, so I stayed in the kitchen with her. She was quiet and I wanted to reassure myself that I wasn't to blame. I busied myself returning the milk and butter to the fridge, putting the jam back in the press, wiping the place mats clean with a cloth. I even pushed the table back against the wall.

Then Mum put her arm round my shoulder and guided me, without speaking, to sit down. Leaning in to me, she started to talk in her softest voice.

'Sheila,' she said. Her voice was low and it caught in her throat.

I hated it when Mum cried, it was embarrassing. It was bad enough when she cried in the sitting room when we were watching a film on television and tried to wipe her eyes and nose without anyone seeing her. Now she was doing it right beside me.

'Sheila,' she said again, gently, to the crown of my head.

I forced myself to look up, dreading the sight of her watery eyes.

'I just want to have a little word with you.' Her voice was almost a whisper.

What have I done now? I wondered. Did Sister Brigid tell her about me not finishing my spelling homework? Did Kevin tell tales about me breaking the back wheel of Action Man's jeep?

'You may have noticed that your Dad hasn't been feeling very well of late. It's nothing to worry about' – she put her hand lightly on my arm – 'it's just his teeth. He's going to his dentist soon and they'll take out a bad bit and some teeth – he'll be fine then. Okay?'

I said nothing.

'I told Catherine and Lucy already and now I'm telling you, Okay?'

'Okay,' I said, unsure of what else I could say.

'I don't think I'll tell Kevin just yet. He's still a bit young. Maybe in a while. So you needn't say anything to him, Okay love?'

'Okay.'

Then she gave me a hug that stopped the blood flow in my arms. I was pinned to the chair. I was sure I heard her muffled sniffles in my hair.

I didn't know where to put this new information. It didn't sink in or change me in any way that I recognised. It sat outside of me – an extra piece of knowledge that I had acquired. It went no further than that.

Sugar

We put sugar on everything.

Occasionally, to add to the ceremony, we had a starter on a Sunday – either a wedge of melon or half a grapefruit each. Regardless of which, every piece was covered in caster sugar and Mum also placed a tiny bowl of sugar in the centre of the table, just in case the slightest note of bitterness was to hit anyone's palate.

In the summertime, we sprinkled sugar on our freshly picked raspberries and strawberries, before smothering them in whipped cream, which also had sugar added to it. At breakfast time, my bowl of porridge was always covered in sugar. And I liked Rice Krispies and Corn Flakes better with lots of sugar sprinkled over. When all the cereal was eaten and a grainy pool of milk remained in my bowl, I checked that Mum wasn't looking, then tilted my head back and gulped down the over-sweetened and crunchy milk, ignoring the dribbles running down my chin and neck and settling in as a stain on my navy school jumper.

Mum and Dad both had heavy hands with sugar when it came to tea and coffee, until one Lent they decided it was time to quit. Mum breezed through those forty days, probably motivated by the extra inches she would lose but also with the assistance of the tiny metal box of Hermesetas she kept beside the coffee jar, one miniscule tablet plopped into every cup. Dad, on the other hand, struggled. Being a purist, he refused any sugar substitute and went cold turkey. After two days, he gave in; he couldn't cope with the withdrawal symptoms and slipped back into his old ways.

When Grandma was minding us one evening, she made 'goodie' for supper. I was treated to it in hushed tones in the kitchen when everyone else was watching television or doing homework. I was being let in on an old family tradition, a touch of decadence – from the war years. She took two slices of bread, buttered them heavily, then held each one in turn above the sugar bowl and sprinkled sugar over them, any excess falling expertly back into the bowl – clearly she had done this before. Then she placed the sweetened bread in a small dish and covered it with hot milk. It was an instant milk pudding, so of course I loved it.

Offal

As most of the meat we ate was well done and required a lot of chewing, kidneys and liver provided a welcome alternative – for me at least. A smooth, soft piece of kidney was often much tastier and more tender than the stewing beef it was cooked with. Only Dad and I liked the kidney pieces that went into Mum's steak and kidney pie, and we happily took donations of kidney bits from the others. Pieces were flung onto our plates from every direction. When someone came across an unwanted piece in their own slice of pie, they'd shout, 'Here's another one – which of you wants it?' Even Mum didn't like kidney, which made me wonder, given her position of control, why she added it to our stews at all. Was it to stretch the meat a little further in order to feed six large stomachs? Was it to please those of us who liked it? Or was it simply to add variety to our dinners?

Similar manoeuvres took place when we had liver. Mum steeped thin slices of lamb's liver in milk for a few hours before dusting each piece lightly with flour and flash frying it in oil. Cooked properly, it was moist with a strong metallic taste and a texture like pâté. Liver and chips was frequently on the midweek menu. Kevin and Lucy piled chips high on their plates, soggy with Heinz Tomato Ketchup. They slipped most of their liver to Catherine and me when Mum was occupied getting more chips from the fryer. Dad loved liver and to keep him quiet, they used to give him some extra too.

There came a day when Dad sat in the midst of our daily dinner shenanigans, very pale and very still. We were having liver, but he had only a small side plate of mashed potato in front of him. A fork rested loosely in his hand, and he looked vacant and disinterested in his food. He'd been to the dentist and had all his back teeth taken out. Through rolls of cotton wool, jammed into each side of his mouth and encrusted with blood, he told me that he could only eat 'mush' for the next few days. He was getting new teeth like Grandma, he said. Then he'd be as right as rain. I was fascinated in a ghoulish way by false teeth, having vague memories of Grandad's in a glass of water by his bedside, and seeing Grandma's slip out onto her chin while she dozed on the sofa with her mouth open. I couldn't wait to see Dad's. In the meantime, I had to make do with staring at his swollen face and neck whenever he looked the other way or slept on the couch.

His mashed potato remained untouched, and silently Mum removed it – its absence less disturbing than its presence. Out of confusion or possibly fear, I'd decided never to question Dad's not eating. I was afraid of Mum's tears if I asked the question out loud, and I was fairly certain I wouldn't want to know the answer anyway. Instead, when he stood up from the table before dessert, I said 'Good night, Dad' in as cheerful a manner as I could – without sounding too happy. It was a tightrope I was walking and I wasn't sure why I was doing it and if I was getting 'it' right.

A momentary silence hung over the table after he closed the door behind him. I listened to him slowly mount the stairs. Maybe someone coughed. Mum surely said something in her best mock-cheerful voice: 'Finish up your dinners now, before I get the dessert.' We conspired silently to ignore Dad's leaving.

Tray-bakes

On Fridays I liked to hang out with Maeve, in her house or mine. It was the start of the weekend, there was no school for two whole days, so we could stay a bit longer in each other's company. These days I preferred being in her house. It was good to escape the hushed atmosphere that had settled over everything at home, despite Mum's efforts at good cheer. 'This is nice, isn't it?' she'd say brightly after we'd watched a film together or had a nice meal. 'Lovely.' 'Yeah.' Our answers would fake a levity we no longer felt. Then gloom returned. Dad was spending a lot of time in bed. We had to be quiet around the house in the middle of the day. If he was not in bed, he was dozing by the fire, wrapped up in his thick maroon dressing gown, his white hairless feet stuck into slippers. Mum said he was recovering from the dentist and that he would be better soon.

In Maeve's house they had cardboard boxes filled with broken biscuits to eat. In what seemed like part of a Roald Dahl plot to me, her uncle worked in a biscuit factory and the O'Reillys were the lucky beneficiaries of many of the rejects from the production line. Sometimes I picked a damaged chocolate ring from the box, only to find there was no biscuit in it at all, just pure chocolate all the way through. Biscuits in our house were kept under lock and key, Mum doling them out as and when she saw fit. These cardboard boxes floated around Maeve's house casually, hands dipping in and out with regularity. There was an amazing freedom and autonomy with treats that I was not used to.

Keen to escape my home, I ran up the road and rang her doorbell to see if she wanted to play. Her Mum opened the door and told me she was out, with Sharon, one of the 'O's from 3B. Kindly she suggested that I go and join them. I knew where Sharon lived, I could have called over but I felt the rejection bitterly. Maeve had moved on, she had done what Sister Joseph had suggested and made new friends. I had not. It was a Friday afternoon and I'd no one to play with. I walked home slowly, an afternoon of colouring and Kevin lying ahead of me. While ordinarily that prospect was not so bad, it felt bleak now that I knew Maeve was having a good time – with someone else.

'Maeve not in?' Mum asked on my return.

'No. What'll I do now?' I mumbled.

'Kevin's inside with his colouring books, why don't you join him?' Mum's response was predictable.

Reluctantly I did as she asked. Kevin was great, but he was just a bit small and he didn't like to play with dolls much. But he'd have to do for now.

Luckily Friday was also *Crackerjack* day and we were allowed put the television on to watch it before the six o'clock news. After a long week at school, this was our little treat. Friday was also the day Mum made a tray-bake. Even with Dad sick, this tradition didn't stop. Perhaps it was because he was sick, that she felt the need to keep at least some treats coming our way.

From the sitting room, I heard the rattle of the weighing scales and the clink of presses being opened and shut. I turned my back on the on-screen chaos, in favour of the kitchen. There I found Mum with one of her many well-used recipes, speckled with yellow smudges and dried-in splashes, spread out on the countertop beside a big bowl, all the ingredients collected and ready.

Mum proudly called me her 'right-hand woman' to neighbours and relatives. I enjoyed the praise and admiration. Unless there were other children present. Then I just wished Mum would shut up and stop making me sound like such a goody two-shoes, a lick and a swot. But I couldn't disguise the fact that I liked working in the kitchen. Scraping carrots, stirring gravy and setting the table were okay jobs to do. But the best job was acting as Mum's assistant during cake-making, or when she was making one of her many tray-bakes. Maeve didn't know what a tray-bake was. She thought it was a stupid word. They were either cakes or biscuits. What's a tray got to do with it? Her mammy didn't make cakes, so what did she know? I didn't let this get in the way of my enjoyment of such delights as chocolate toffee slices, flapjacks, almond slices, apple slices, melting moments, florentines, chocolate biscuit cake, shortbread. Mum even made her own Jaffa cakes, ginger biscuits and chocolate-chip cookies.

I sidled in, sneaked a look in the bowl and at the scattered ingredients and made a mental assessment of the type of finger-licking and bowl-scraping I would be doing. I asked if I could help.

'Oh would you grease that tin, love, please?' Mum replied.

Yuck! The worst job! I couldn't complain. I couldn't always get the nice jobs. So I spread slimy margarine all over the inside of the blackened tray, even right into the corners with my fingertips, trying not to get them too greasy.

Sometimes Mum let me crack eggs into bowls of half-made Madeira mixture and each time she turned to put the shells in the bin, I dipped my finger deep into the centre of the raw mixture and pulled out as large a dollop as it would hold. If I arrived too late in the kitchen, the only help I could offer was to spread the mixture into the tin. This often worked in my favour, as the amount of wooden-spoon-sucking I got to do was totally disproportionate to the amount of assistance provided.

From my place at her elbow I watched Mum's hands work skilfully with each different mixture: gentle folding with a metal spoon for one; vigorous pounding with a wooden spoon for another; delicately transforming a lump of butter and flour into the finest crumbs for pastry with her fingertips. Her hands were remarkable.

'I've awful old hands,' she said when she saw me looking at them. 'I didn't want anyone to look at them when I was playing piano or typing.' She held them in front of her and looked at them in disgust.

They were large, it was true, with big knuckles that meant she had to have her wedding and engagement rings specially sized to fit. Her poor circulation left them purple a lot of the time. She suffered from deep, sore cracks around her finger-tips when the weather turned bad. In fact, she could predict a change in the weather when her fingertips started to split. I didn't care what they looked like. What she did with them was pure magic. They were as defining a part of her as her striking grey hair and her loud witchy laugh.

Together we worked to finish the tray-bake, see it safely into the oven. And out of a sense of fair play, I helped with the washing-up too, before returning to the television. Watching the remainder of *Crackerjack* with Kevin, I listened out for the rattle of the oven-timer. When it sounded, I dashed into the kitchen and watched in awe as Mum took the tray-bake out of the oven. I'd an agonising wait while it cooled in its tin, was cut into slices, and was lifted one piece at a time onto the wire rack to let cool a little more. It was sheer torture.

Mum felt pity for me and relented. She took a small slice and cut it in two. 'It's a bit broken anyway,' she whispered, passing one half to me and popping the other half into her mouth.

In silence we shared the delicious, still-warm tray-bake, standing by the kitchen countertop, too impatient to be seated.

Mould

There was something brave about the way Grandma appraised a block of cheese that had lingered for too long in her fridge. She held it firmly in her gnarled, arthritic hands and examined it thoroughly on all sides. Then she took her sharpest knife and cut only the thinnest of slices off each side to remove all of the mould yet spare as much of the cheese as possible. She'd eat the rest of the block with abandon. She treated fuzzy bread, pots of mouldy jam, and rotten fruit in the same casual manner. Cut, scoop or chop off the offending mould and enjoy what's left. 'What won't kill you will only make you stronger' was her attitude. This she also declared as she picked dropped food off the floor before popping it into her mouth.

Mum inherited this devil-may-care approach to mould. She never minded having the slice of bread where the blue bit had to be cut off; she kept the half-rotten apple for herself and gave me the firm one. But it was when mould passed from Grandma's house into ours that Mum got annoyed. This happened when Grandma was going on her annual visit to London to see her daughter, Aunty Mary.

When Mum and I arrived at Grandma's house to drive her to the airport, she was packed and ready to go, standing by the open front door. Her small suitcase contained, alongside the usual, a few well-wrapped bags of rashers, sausages and tea bags, and a tea-brack she had made herself. Resting against her suitcase was a white plastic bag. As Mum loaded her case into the car, Grandma handed me the plastic bag. 'Make sure you put those in the fridge when you get home,' she said.

Saying goodbye at the departure gates, Grandma squeezed my face between the palms of her trembling hands and looked at me so closely I could smell her old-lady funk and see the dusting of face-powder clinging to the large pores of her nose. Then she hugged her daughter to her tightly as they both sniffled into each other's collars. Carefully, with both Mum and I helping, Grandma got onto the little airport golf cart. Back to back with the driver she sat. As the cart pulled away she placed her handbag safely on her lap and waved goodbye to us until we could no longer see her. We saw the funny side of this scene and shared a giggle as Grandma shrank in the distance.

When we got home, I emptied the contents of the bag onto the kitchen table:

An opened packet of Philadelphia Cream Cheese – under the tinfoil was a thick growth of green fuzz.

A few rashers wrapped in cling film – their colour a little pallid and when lifted and sniffed, the smell sent Mum reeling.

A Yoplait yoghurt almost two weeks beyond its sell-by date. Even so, I couldn't resist sticking a teaspoon in and giving it a try. The fizzy sensation that hopped off my tongue told me all was not right with it.

Two black bananas, soft and very pungent. There was no way I was going to eat either of them.

In an old glacé cherry carton were some Bachelors Beans – we were a 'Beanz Meanz Heinz' household – that had turned dark brown and a hard crust had formed on them.

Mum sighed heavily as she inspected Grandma's fridge contents. 'As if I don't have enough on my plate!' she said.
Clunk, thump, thud – each item landed heavily in our kitchen bin.
Grandma, on the other hand, who hated waste, had left for England with an easy conscience, knowing her leftovers had found a new home. She never discovered where they ended up. Instead, when she phoned that night from England to say she had arrived safely, she was thanked for her bounty. When she returned a few days later, Mum had stocked her fridge and pantry with fresh fruit, milk, bread, eggs; enough essentials to 'get her started'. Grandma, I thought, did very well out of this exchange.

Cadbury's Miniatures

In England they had things that we didn't have in Ireland. They had chocolate bars called Double Deckers; their Cadbury's bars came in chunkier, longer shapes that were much nicer to bite into; there were Battenburg cakes, Foxes biscuits, orange- and mint-flavoured Club Milks. There was plenty for Grandma to choose from when deciding what to bring home as presents.

Top of my list was the wallet-sized purple box of Cadbury's Miniatures. Inside the cardboard box were individually wrapped squares of heavenly milk chocolate. It was thrilling to eat an entire chocolate bar in a single bite. A normal bar of chunky chocolate may have provided more in the way of chocolate, but I wanted the added experience of being Gulliver, a giant girl making a chocolate bar look minuscule in the palm of her hand. I liked to put one in Sindy's plastic hand too, it was the perfect size for her. I ate them one by one until my lap was littered with purple and silver wrappers.

Grandma brought home a five-pack of Double Deckers just for Dad – they were his favourite. Mum took them quietly from her and put them up high in the sitting room unit, in a press only she could reach. She was keeping them until Dad's appetite returned.

After Grandma left for the evening and all my chocolate was gone, I needed a little reassurance about Dad. The last time he received such bounty from England, he went into the kitchen and took the carving knife out and cut one of his bars into four equal pieces, one for each of us to savour, while he had a whole bar all to himself. This time he showed no interest in them. He smiled wanly at Grandma in thanks. I wanted some answers. I wanted it explained to me about his moods and his visit to the dentist and whether false teeth would cure him or not. But who could I ask? Mum was far too emotional. When she told me about Dad, it made me uncomfortable; her sniffles and too-tight hugs were not what I needed. She had embarrassed me in front of an empty kitchen. I couldn't risk that again.

I had no choice but to turn to my big sisters. They had been allowed go into town on the bus without Mum. Catherine had been to a disco in school. They giggled about boys. I assumed that their greater experience of the world gave them a head-start on me. They were bound to have superior knowledge of medical matters and some insight into Dad's condition. So on my way to bed that night I tapped lightly on their bedroom door and went inside. They were both stretched out with their heads at the foot of their beds, reading books. They looked up and stared blankly at me, unsure of how to react to my perplexing presence within their sanctuary.

'Lucy?' Always more approachable than Catherine.

'Hmmm?'

'Can I ask you something?'

'Hmmm?'

'What's wrong with Dad? He looks old. He doesn't eat or go to work any more. Do you know?'

'It's his teeth, silly,' she said, tutting at me and throwing her eyes up to heaven for Catherine's amusement.

They both shrugged their shoulders at my ignorance. I didn't care about being ridiculed; I wanted to get to the bottom of the problem and would suffer their condescension if I had to.

'Are you sure?' I persisted. 'He still hasn't eaten in ages and it's only mash he gets.'

'Of course I'm sure,' Lucy said. 'That's what Mum told us. It'll take time for his mouth to get better and then he'll get his falsies so he can eat and talk and stuff. Now go to bed and stop annoying us.'

She returned to reading her book. I was dismissed. I was not reassured. But there was no one else I could turn to.

Campbell's Meatballs

Aunty Teresa took Kevin and me back to Cashel with her for a weekend. She told us in the car on the drive down that our mum needed a break. We liked Aunty Teresa. Not only was she generous with the bags of boiled sweets she kept in her handbag and the chocolate bars she stored in her kitchen, but she was the best tickler ever. She made me scream and cry all at once with the pain and joy of the tickles she inflicted on my tummy, my ribs, my arms and my back. I wriggled and screamed under her hands; her fingers instruments of delicious torture. No one else tickled like Aunty Teresa. So it was without reluctance that I got into her tiny green Mini and let her take us to Cashel.

Aunty Teresa was the daughter who had stayed at home to look after her deaf mother, ailing aunt and elderly father. Now they were all gone and she lived alone in the family home. Dad had shown me the small house, at the foot of The Rock, in which he was born. The house we were staying in was the one in which he had spent most of his childhood. It was on the main street of the town, right at the heart of the action, beside the entrance to the grand hotel, opposite several pubs and only down the road from Burke's sweet shop. Very tall and narrow, it was a house with so many stairs winding up through its centre that I lost count.

There was an unused shop at the front of the house, where Dad's mother had run a small grocery business. The shop had long been abandoned but the fixtures and fittings were still in place. Kevin and I liked to lift up the counter and walk in behind, examining the empty shelves that were still lined with old newspapers. We played shop with a few tins and packets stolen from Aunty Teresa's kitchen, taking turns at being customer and shopkeeper.

The rest of the house comprised another three floors – it was very confusing. The sitting room was upstairs and one bedroom was on the same level as it; then the bathroom was above this and there were more bedrooms up higher again. I could never remember where the toilet was and inevitably barged into Aunty Teresa's bedroom, which was either a floor above or below it.

Aunty Teresa thought she was giving us a treat on our first night when she served up tinned Campbell's Meatballs for dinner. Mum never served an entire meal from a tin; a few peas, some salmon for a salad, or Spam when we were camping, but an entire meal, never. So Aunty Teresa was doing her own thing, spoiling us a little with this foreign dish. Served warm in a cereal bowl, the red sauce was sweet and the meat was rubbery. It had odd flavours. Before leaving home, Kevin and I had been warned by Mum to clean our plates and remember our manners, so we ate everything Aunty Teresa put in front of us.

That night I awoke from my sleep with a tummy ache. I knew something was wrong. I needed to go to the toilet. I wanted to be sick. But where was the toilet? Was it just a few steps across the hall or did I have to go up, or was it down, a flight of stairs? I lay in the bed beside Kevin, who was fast asleep, and wondered if I should waken Aunty Teresa and ask for help. I was very confused. But before I could climb over Kevin, it was too late. I heaved involuntarily and the warm red contents of my stomach splashed all over Kevin and our bed. Kevin woke up screaming. I started crying.

Aunty Teresa burst into our room. She stood at the door, her hairnet pinned down, securing every strand and curl in its rightful place. Her face was glistening with the Pond's Cold Cream she gently massaged into her skin morning and night. She held her dressing gown tightly across her chest. She didn't show revulsion or get cross, instead she started to laugh her warm infectious laugh. She couldn't stop herself. She held her stomach tightly in her efforts to stop but she just laughed more and more. Her unexpected reaction stopped our wailing. We sat on our soggy bed and I started to giggle a little too – I was feeling better already. Kevin almost saw the funny side of it.

When she recovered her composure, Aunty Teresa got us out of the bed and stripped Kevin of his pyjamas. She wiped him clean and put on his day clothes – there were no spare pyjamas lying around her house. She got me a drink of water and told us to wait in the sitting room next door. We sat shivering on the old chaise longue in the darkened room while she made up our bed. Then she tucked us in again and kissed us firmly on our cheeks, through a final wave of her laughter. Aunty Teresa got much pleasure from recounting this story on our return to Dublin.

Onion Sandwiches

Mum loosened her grip on the kitchen a little on Saturdays. Usually she allowed us to make our own breakfasts and lunches. She may have suggested that there was ham in the fridge or plenty of Calvita cheese and crackers, but she let us get on with it as a form of learning exercise. So after a morning spent watching *Swap Shop* and Tarzan movies, it was time for lunch.

I chose to ignore the saucepan of Erin potato soup Mum had left on the cooker. I was going to make myself Dad's favourite – an onion sandwich. This was one of the few 'meals' Dad made and he only got the opportunity to do so on a Saturday. He enjoyed rekindling his bachelor days and striking out for culinary independence every once in a while. In any case, Mum refused to make what she considered a revolting idea for a sandwich.

I watched in fascination the first time I ever saw him make one. His preparation in all tasks, whether it was DIY, gardening or sandwich-making, was meticulous and painfully slow – the exact opposite of Mum's frantic and blindingly fast scraping, chopping and mixing. When it came to peeling an onion, a tedious task for most people, Dad ensured that the shiny outer skin, and *only* the outer skin, was removed. He considered it a failure and wasteful if

he stripped away a layer of edible flesh. So with the tip of a small sharp knife, he broke the outer skin of the onion and chipped away patiently at it until every last fleck of skin was on the chopping board and he held only a clean, white and naked onion in his hand. He placed two slices of white bread flat on the bread board and spread margarine thinly out to every corner, missing nothing. Holding the onion high, he did not take his eyes off the carving knife as it slid through the flesh. The slices were so thin I could see the light from the kitchen window through each one. Four slices of onion covered one slice of bread and a fifth slice was chopped finely and used to shore up any gaps. He didn't even use a quarter of an onion to make an entire sandwich. He sprinkled plenty of salt and white pepper over the onion, before gently pressing down the top slice of bread and cutting the sandwich neatly in two. Then he sat at the table with his bachelor meal and a tall glass of milk.

I looked on in disgust and horror as Dad raised the sandwich to his mouth. I made involuntary gagging noises when he took his first bite.

He got irritated. 'Don't say it's disgusting until you've tried it!' he snapped.

He was right. I felt foolish and silly, and so in an attempt to save face with Dad, I rose to his challenge and asked for a bite. How bad could it be?

'You can have this,' he said, and smiled as he passed me the other half of his sandwich. He wasn't going to let me off with a mere bite.

'Thanks,' I said in my most nonchalant voice.

I didn't hesitate. I didn't want to seem weak. I bit straight into it.

The onion sandwich was a revelation. My teeth met with soft bread, a hint of grease, the clean crunch of the juicy onion and gritty salt. It had a nice bite. There was a good combination of textures in that simple sandwich. It was similar to the Tayto sandwich – Cheese & Onion crisps squashed down and crushed into delicious pieces between two slices of buttered bread. I became an onion sandwich convert there and then. Dad was delighted to see that he, too, could pass on some 'recipes' to his children.

And so, as he lay asleep upstairs in his darkened room that Saturday, as a form of morose homage to him, I made myself an onion sandwich. It was my way of feeling close to him. My slices of onion were thicker, my butter was applied in lumps, and I didn't add pepper, but together with a big glass of milk it made a completely satisfying meal that resonated with me all afternoon, and kept me belching until tea time.

Fillamillu

Grandma's hearing degenerated steadily. After much persuading, she relented and got a hearing aid. Wearing it irritated her. It made sonic feedback noises most of the time. We suspected this was when its battery was running low. When the high-pitched screeching started, Grandma reached behind her ear and turned it off. She hated spending money on new batteries, so most of the time its purpose was decorative and, more importantly for Grandma, being seen to wear it kept her concerned children off her back. At night-time she wore giant headphones plugged into her television set so that she could hear it without disturbing the neighbours. When I tried to have a conversation with her, I shouted until my face turned red. Sometimes I got frustrated repeating myself and shortened my sentences and my conversations with her. At other times the consequences of her deafness were a source of much amusement both to us and to her, as she didn't take herself too seriously.

On Sundays, after the scones and tea and when Maudie had gone back to Grantham Street, Grandma went to Uncle Pat's, Aunty Eileen's, or to our house for dinner. There was an unspoken and casual arrangement between her children and their spouses: Grandma was to be with her offspring for the rest of the day. She was brought from Ranelagh to suburbia, and entertained and fed before being dropped home, just in time for the nine o'clock news. It was a system that worked well.

On the Sunday nights that Grandma was absent from our house, she phoned at ten to nine precisely to speak to Mum; no one but Mum moved to answer the phone – what was the point? The only sounds I heard coming from the hall were Mum's patient 'Yes … Yes … Right … Really? … Is that so? … Yes …' as Grandma regaled her daughter with the events of the day.

In the sitting room I silently stared at the screen, not paying attention to the news, just glad not to be in bed with nothing but a Monday morning to look forward to. I hoped that if I was quiet and caused no trouble, Dad would stay asleep and not wake up to see me and Kevin still downstairs after nine o'clock. It had worked so far.

At a quarter past nine one particular Sunday Mum returned to the sitting room. 'My God!' she exclaimed, exasperated. 'Every little fiddle faddle! I have to hear every detail about her day. And look, now I've missed the news.'

She plonked herself back down on the sofa and, in turn, recounted to us, over the sound of the closing news sum- mary and weather forecast, each minute detail of Grandma's day. How Pat's house was looking; how the DIY he was undertaking in the bathroom was progressing; what his two boys were doing and what they said; what Mary, Pat's wife, was wearing. The meal, being her favourite part of the ritual, Grandma had described in even greater detail. The lasagne was perfect: firm but not hard; not too dry nor too runny; it held the square shape of the portion as Mary served it; the baked potatoes were lovely and floury, with a dollop of sour cream melting in the cross at the centre. She only ate a small amount of salad. But knowing Grandma's sweet tooth, Mary had saved her best for last and spoiled her mother-in-law with an impressive new Italian dessert.

Pleased to have a funny anecdote that might lift the mood in the room, Mum told us all about this delicious dish. About the layers of creamy, cheesy mixture on top of the layers of sponge fingers dipped in coffee laced with alcohol, all beautifully arranged and on view in Mary's glass serving bowl. There was a dusting of chocolate powder on top, or was it Cadbury's Flake? Grandma couldn't remember. It had chilled all afternoon in the fridge and was cool and spongy and wickedly boozy to eat. Grandma had seconds, with fresh cream on the side, on both occasions. It was very professional-looking, she said. But the best about it all was the name that Grandma had misheard – Fillamillu.

Mum got a faint chuckle out of each of her four children on the recounting of this story – having never tasted tiramisu, the joke meant little to us, though we laughed for her sake. Dad barely lifted an eyelid during its telling. Mum glared over at him, irritated that he had neither listened nor found it funny.

'Right now, you pair, off to bed with you. It's way past your bedtime,' she said.

The atmosphere reverted, just like that.

The Drinks Cabinet

Very little alcohol was consumed in our house. Mum poured herself a solitary glass of sherry while preparing the Sunday roast and the Christmas turkey. This tiny glass she kept by her side, taking it with her as she moved from surface to surface around the kitchen. A drop of alcohol had never passed my father's lips, the brass Pioneer pin he wore on his lapel and moved from jacket to jacket bore testimony to his abstinence, so no other alcoholic beverage was consumed most weeks.

The 'drinks cabinet' was a press in a unit that Dad built, which fitted snugly into the alcove in our sitting room. On the bottom shelf sat our set of encyclopaedias – A to Z lined across the width of the unit, with just enough room for a Philip's Atlas at the end. I was encouraged – forced, I should say – to use these books when I had a question about geography, nature, science or music. 'You'll remember it better if you look it up yourself' was the annoying mantra Mum and Dad sing-songed if I moaned at the prospect of having to work for the answer. (It never occurred to me that they might not know the answer.) On the next shelf up were some old novels by A.J. Cronin and Daphne Du Maurier, and a few John F. Kennedy biographies. This is where our Oxford English Dictionary and our Irish–English dictionary by Tomás De Bhaldraithe sat. Above this was open shelving filled with photos of our extended family, and the drinks cabinet.

When visitors called, once greetings were over and they were seated, the door to the drinks cabinet was let down, like a drawbridge over a castle moat. It was the only door in the house that opened like that. There was an unusual smell inside the cabinet, too – an old, sweet and damp smell. All the drinks were on display so that guests could take their pick. There were always large bottles of Paddy's Irish Whiskey, Martini, Harvey's Bristol Cream and Gordon's Gin. (Never one to let anything go to waste, Dad made several lamp shades from empty whiskey bottles of curious shapes. A Dimple Scotch Whisky bottle sat in my bedroom for years. Through the clear glass I could see the wire enter from a tiny bored hole in the base of the bottle and travel on up through the main cavity into the light bulb. I thought it was ingenious.)

Around these large bottles were fitted numerous toy-like bottles of rum, brandy, Curaçao and other odd-sounding potions, as well as bottles shaped like musical instruments and churches, which Mum and Dad received as gifts from abroad. These were never opened. On a shelf above all the alcohol sat the glassware. There were a few mismatched Waterford crystal glasses – wedding presents – but never a complete set.

With visitors in the house, Mum had a Martini, maybe two. She liked it mixed with TK White Lemonade and ice. Some guests went straight for the whiskey and water, while the sophisticates from London always asked for a G&T. On such occasions, the odd glass of 'mineral' did it for Dad. To whet his appetite, Mum now regularly included huge bottles of Cidona, Club Orange and red lemonade in her shopping – 'for Dad' we were told. He liked to sip at different drinks all day and sugary ones were more appealing to him. They were lined up on a high shelf in the cold garage for Dad to drink his way through or until guests arrived. When we had visitors, we children were allowed to enjoy a glass of mineral, too.

Cidona made me feel grown up. There was something mature about the look and smell of this drink. I shook my glass and let the ice cubes clink off the sides. I was a femme fatale from a Hollywood movie, knocking back strong liquor that had been poured over ice from a silver shaker. It tasted as if it was something I shouldn't be drinking. It definitely didn't taste like other drinks for kids. It was the fizzy drink of choice for the discerning child.

Christmas Cake

The learning load in school eased off. I counted down the days left until the Christmas holidays. We lit all three of the purple advent candles; we made yards of paper chains to hang around the prefab, in a vain attempt at brightening it up; and we learned 'Silent Night' in German. No German had ever been taught in our school, and none of the teachers knew how to speak it, but phonetically we learnt 'Schteel-a-gay Nacht, Hile-a-gay Nacht'. We even sang it in harmony when a few of the classes got together in the hall and our voices filled its hollow space.

Our Christmas tree wasn't up yet. There was no festive atmosphere at home. I saw the lights shimmering on Maeve's tree through the bubbly pane of glass beside her front door as we approached her house. It was a fat tree adorned with thick scarves of tinsel and multicoloured balls. The sight of it made me yearn for one in our hallway too. I wanted to smell the sweet pine and touch my favourite decoration – a blue sparkling sparrow – and place it high on a branch where I could see it as I climbed the stairs.

Mum had never bought a Christmas tree on her own before, she couldn't fit it into the car, she didn't know how much to pay – there were many reasons why our house was the only one on the road with no tree visible.

But when Mum opened the front door to greet me on the last day of school, the house was filled with the smells of Christmas. Lying across the hall was a small, naked but very fragrant tree, on the thin side, it had to be admitted, but a tree all the same. Our boxes of decorations were down from the attic and stacked up beside it. And wafting up the hall was a delicious smell that made me giddy inside. I skipped into the kitchen and there, in her biggest earthenware bowl, Mum was steeping fruit for the Christmas cake. Raisins, sultanas, currants, glacé cherries, dates – they were all bathing in a decadent mixture of whiskey and orange zest and juice. The wizened fruit was soaking up the liquid, slowly getting plump and glossy. I smelled the wonderful aroma of nutmeg, mixed spice and cinnamon.

On the table were strips of grease-proof paper. Mum was muttering and 'damning' away to herself as she cut out circles and strips to line the inside of her blackened cake tin. She hated this fiddly job but her notes from the previous year reminded her that her cake had burned, and she had to be extra careful today. On the countertop, around the weighing scales, was every bowl we possessed, each one filled with a different ingredient. Ground almonds, chopped walnuts, grated lemon and orange zest, grated apple and half a dozen eggs.

Usually Mum made 'The Cake' during the midterm break, but this year November came and went, December was more than half over, and Christmas cake or Christmas pudding hadn't been mentioned. At the last minute Mum was trying to make Christmas normal, so she had set aside this afternoon to make her cake.

I liked stirring the mixture, tasting it and watching as it changed colour and consistency with the addition of each new ingredient. I wasn't strong enough to stir it for long, though. When I tired, the only thing I could do to stay involved in this special ritual was tip each ingredient from the weighing scales into the bowl. This was not a very responsible job, but I understood that when it came to the Christmas cake, I was lucky to be involved at all. For making the Christmas cake made Mum anxious; it was a complex and delicate operation and mistakes could not be tolerated.

The cake baked in the oven for what seemed like an entire day. Its fragrance permeated every corner of the house, upstairs and down. It was taken out of the oven several times, prodded deeply with a knitting needle and then returned for further cooking. When it was finally judged to be cooked, had several hours to cool and was unwrapped from its papery nest, Mum made her initial assessment. She would judge it either a disaster or perfect. There was no other option. In previous years she wrapped the cake in fresh layers of paper and stored it under her bed, taking it downstairs every week to spear it again with her knitting needle and douse it with whiskey. With only four days to go until Christmas, that ritual was dropped this year.

Mum blared up her Bing Crosby and Nat King Cole festive discs on her 3-in-1 record player as she moved about the house doing the domestic chores associated with Christmas – decorating the skinny tree, hanging the Christmas cards on string over the fireplace, icing the cake – enthusiastically helped by me and Kevin. The music played loudly and I took great pleasure in her booming rendition of

'Santa Claus is Coming to Town', as she sang along with Bing Crosby and the Andrews Sisters. Even Catherine and Lucy didn't shout at Mum to 'Pleeease turn it down!', as they would have done in years gone by.

Dad drifted from the sitting room to his bedroom. His bony frame protruded through the scratchy thick wool of his dressing gown as he shuffled from one room to the other. His false teeth had not helped him to get better. He loved Bing Crosby and I hoped that he was smiling, above in his bed, as Mum turned up the record player when Bing sang 'Galway Bay', 'Swinging on a Star' and 'McNamara's Band' – songs they both enjoyed together.

After decorating the tree, the next best job was icing the cake. Mum's almond icing was moist and very thick. She had two tricks that made her icing the best ever. The first was to add a small amount of glycerine to keep it soft. The second seemed quite bizarre to me. To make her icing a brilliant white, she added a few drops of laundry blue. Under the cold tap, she lightly rinsed a rag containing this magic blue, knotted somewhere inside it, then squeezed it over the icing bowl until several drops, the colour of doll's eyes, splashed onto her white icing mix. Then she whipped it into the mixture and repeated the process until she was convinced her icing was a blinding white. This process seemed to me a bit unsanitary. To squeeze a dirty rag into our food? I wondered how we never got sick from it.

For a few years, with my encouragement, the cake decorations were very ornate, with fancy trellis work and tiny patterns around the sides. Mum had an old metal icing pump that had numerous different nozzles, which I screwed onto the top. Then I stuck my fingers and thumb through the red plastic rings and steadily applied pressure, squeezing the icing through in waves and curlicues. I enjoyed the repetition and the precision this task required. However, under time and patience constraints, Mum decided this year that she was finished with humouring me. This Christmas she was going back to her favourite design – the snow storm. She let me help with it, though, and I enjoyed lifting the icing into messy peaks with the flat of a knife. On the top, I stuck Santa Claus and a few other festive creatures, and Mum tied a wide red ribbon around the cake to hide the un-iced sides.

The cake sat, fully dressed, on the dining table for the last days before Christmas, and that is where I went to look at it when I wanted to admire it. I tapped gently on the icing to hear the tiny noise my nail made on its hardening surface. I stared at the miniature Santa, the robin that was twice his size and the funny green tree, with icing from Christmases past still clinging to its branches, all haphazardly stuck on the cake. I thought it was wonderful. I couldn't wait for the

ceremony of cutting the cake on Christmas Eve when Mum carried it into the kitchen, after an evening tea of warm baked ham on fresh white bread.

If only I liked Christmas cake. I wished I could like it. Every year I tasted a bit in the hope of liking it. Every year I spat it out onto my red serviette. I liked the almond icing and the white icing, but to me the cake itself was terrible. Visitors were always offered some and I watched them enjoy it. Dad loved it and it's true to say that he ate most of it. On St Stephen's Day he was allowed to be reckless in the kitchen. He'd finish his modest breakfast of one Weetabix with warm milk and then, with a wry smile, he'd lift the carefully wrapped cake off the trolley, where it remained during its short lifespan, and cut himself a thick slice. Without getting a plate or even a serviette to put it on – those were Mum's niceties – he'd devour the slice, standing up, in two joyous mouthfuls. He knew he was being wicked and loved every moment of it. Mum indulged his rare lapse into gluttony; after all, she was receiving a well-deserved compliment, in actions if not in words.

When Dad attempted to cut a slice on subsequent mornings all romanticism was gone, and he was told in Mum's most practical voice that he had to watch his health, his weight, his heart. However, he usually found plenty of other opportunities to eat Christmas cake and bit by fruity bit. Dad, with some assistance from visitors, made his way through the entire ten-inch square.

Not this year.

The Christmas cake remained unopened and uneaten on the trolley when Dad went into hospital in January.

The Roast

Dad left for the hospital on a Sunday afternoon – 'so he would be seen to first thing on Monday morning,' Mum said. We each hugged him goodbye. He squeezed me very tightly. He had watery eyes. Mum packed him into the car and they drove off in the darkening evening. Grandma shut the door after them and ushered us back into the safety of the sitting room. We were going to get a roast this Sunday as a feeble form of compensation, as a way of keeping routines going, keeping life normal.

The roast was the meal event of the week. Its preparation and consumption had been the same every Sunday for years. Preparation would start early on Sunday morning. Before Mass, Mum peeled vast piles of potatoes and left them in her largest saucepan covered in cold water; she scraped bags of carrots; she organised bowls, the gravy boat, trays, plates and serving dishes around the oven where they would get warm when the oven came on (she timed it to switch on while we were out). Later in the afternoon, when we returned from a reluctant (on my part) walk in the Dublin Mountains or Killiney Head, the cooking began in earnest. I could hear the work from the sitting room, where mouth-watering smells reached me as I watched television.

Around six o'clock, Dad would be called to the kitchen. A

minute later I'd see him walking up the back garden into the shed, where he sharpened the carving knife on his sharpening stone. Then he'd return to the kitchen and start to carve the meat. No bone was too knuckly, no joint too gristly for Dad and his newly sharpened knife. Even Mum's dry brown beef, which had turned crunchy and black on the outside after most of the day in the oven, cut easily into razor-thin slices under Dad's knife.

Mum would call the rest of us in several minutes before she served dinner. It took us time, and her increasingly angry calls, to drag ourselves away from the television, our bedrooms or whatever it was we were doing. I'd enter the steamed-up kitchen, with Mum running back and forth from sink to cooker to table and sink again. Draining, stirring, mashing, glazing – all done at the last minute, all done single-handedly.

The first five minutes at the table were always chaotic, as we all tried to serve ourselves and each other at once, passing dishes, bowls and the gravy boat around until every plate was loaded. A mini-Christmas every week. Calmness would then descend as we tucked in and devoured our dinners.

The well-cooked meat, dry and curling slightly at the edges, would be served with two vegetables from Mum's repertoire – cauliflower with cheese sauce (a sauce so dense it completely disguised the rustic taste of cauliflower); carrots, sometimes smothered in thick parsley sauce; peas; carrots and parsnips mashed together; green beans (with pieces of rasher added to give the soggy strings a modicum of flavour); or Brussels sprouts. These vegetables were bubbled and boiled until all life was drained from them. If there was the faintest bite left in the vegetables, someone was sure to complain. 'These vegetables are raw!' And Mum would apologise. There were always more than enough potatoes to go around – two roast for everyone (three for Dad) and then some extra, mashed, for the very hungry. All served piping hot with a boat of dark brown Bisto gravy and any other necessary titbits: apple sauce with pork, stuffing with chicken, mint jelly with lamb and, occasionally, Yorkshire puddings with beef.

The meal may have taken most of the day to prepare but it never took us more than ten minutes to wolf it down. We had big appetites and rose easily to the challenge of large portions and plates piled high. There was even the option of second helpings if anyone wanted, which most of us did. The idea of getting only one plate of food to eat was anathema to us. 'Who'll have the last bit of breast?' or 'It won't be the same tomorrow' was what Mum said as she placed the last morsels of food on our cleared plates. And I ate it all, regardless of how much I had eaten already or how tight the skin was stretching across my belly.

I also had to remember to leave room for dessert, as Mum always went that extra mile on Sunday. Milk puddings might do during the week, but Sunday meant trifle, mousse or pavlova – a dessert with a little X factor.

Once the dinner plates were removed to the sink, Mum presented her dessert. This was where her real talents in the kitchen lay. In the creation of all things rich and sweet, she reigned supreme. She never had to fish for compliments during this course, as unmistakable noises of pleasure spontaneously escaped from us. A cacophony of *hmmms* and *ahhhhs* told Mum how much we were enjoying it. And the fight for the last piece said it all.

At seventy-eight years of age, Grandma had cooked many kinds of roast in her day but it was a long time since she had cooked one for a whole family. As all four of us sat watching *Little House on the Prairie* the day Dad went into hospital, we listened to Grandma moving about our kitchen, unfamiliar to her, opening and closing presses and drawers in obvious confusion. While Mum had prepared the potatoes and put the chicken in the oven before leaving, Grandma was left to prepare the vegetables and put it all together. Catherine and Lucy weren't usually interested in offering any culinary help but each of them stuck their heads around the kitchen door and asked Grandma if she was okay. She said she was fine. I was eager to help her but I was not skilled enough to be of much use. So after standing idly behind her at the cooker for a few minutes, I left her alone and returned to the hushed sitting room. None of us knew exactly the right thing to do, so we kept the volume on the television low and half watched it, while half listening to Grandma's slower movements around the kitchen.

We'd never had a roast chicken without Mum and Dad before and I felt strange and lonely sitting around the table laden with food, without them present. Grandma had done her best to carve the chicken, two drumsticks were discernible on a serving plate but were surrounded by shredded pieces of white and brown meat all mixed up and slick with fatty juices. Carrots, cut in rounds and not in strips the way Mum prepared them, were glistening from the copious amount of melted butter that dripped over them. The roast potatoes, while abundant, were pale and soft, rather than the golden crispiness of Mum's. The gravy was cloudy and a light brown colour, clearly no Bisto had been used in its making. We each sat politely around the display of food, and the usual mad interweaving of reaching arms was absent, as we waited for Grandma to signal that it was okay to start serving ourselves. As soon as she told us to tuck in, we made a start, but with an unusual reserve.

It was a quiet roast. We answered Grandma's questions, but spoke little otherwise. I was thinking of Dad. He was in hospital and not just for one night. He was having an operation. It was serious. Mum's face and his hugs told me so.

I didn't feel like second helpings. Grandma filled a plate with a bit of everything for Mum, covered it with the lid of a saucepan and placed it in the oven to keep warm. Each of the leftovers she plated individually and put in the fridge. There was no dessert and I didn't mind. I took a few biscuits into the sitting room and watched a last bit of telly for some distraction, hoping Mum would get home before I had to go to bed.

I was drifting off to sleep when I heard the front door gently click shut. Mentally I was getting up to go downstairs and see Mum but the next time I opened my eyes it was Monday morning.

Kevin's Birthday Tea

Kevin turned eight on the 20th of January 1980. Dad was not home yet and we had not seen him since he left, so Kevin had to celebrate his birthday without him. The enthusiasm for a party was always somewhat dimmer in January, the festivities of Christmas still lingering. But Kevin wasn't too bothered – once he got his *Star Wars* action figures, he was happy. Despite the bad timing, Mum prepared the usual 'spread' for Kevin's birthday tea. The menu was fixed. It never varied. That's what each of us wanted and that's what each of us got.

SAVOURY MENU FOR BIRTHDAY TEA PARTY

HAM SANDWICHES; EGG SANDWICHES

VOL-AU-VENTS
(Chicken for the children; mushroom for the adults)

COCKTAIL SAUSAGES
(Glistening straight from the oven with cocktail sticks poking out in every direction)

DOUBLE-DECKER SANDWICHES

As soon as Mum heard of double-decker sandwiches, they became a staple at birthday teas. They were made using four slices of bread: cottage cheese spread on one, Heinz Sandwich Spread on the second, and mashed hard-boiled egg on the third. The fourth slice was placed on top. These sandwiches were cut into long thin fingers, which instantly made them special and sophisticated, a bit like sandwiches cut into triangles with no crusts. The overriding taste was of Heinz Sandwich Spread. Its vinegar kick overwhelmed the mild moistness of the cottage cheese and even managed to disguise the pungent hard-boiled egg.

For my first helping, I filled up my paper plate – birthday parties were the only time Mum used paper plates – with a bit of everything: one of each kind of sandwich, a chicken vol-au-vent, and as many sausages as I could spear onto the same cocktail stick. A big jug of Miwadi diluted orange stood in the middle of the table and I gulped at several cups of this to help wash down all the lovely stodge. My second helping was less ambitious, consisting of just one double-decker and a few sausages. When our pace had slowed to a halt and all the sausages were gone, Mum cleared away the plates and bowls in preparation for the next round.

SWEET MENU FOR BIRTHDAY TEA PARTY

MERINGUES
(So light, you couldn't feel their weight in your palm.
When they were stuck together with cream, they sparkled
in their paper cases. Their delicacy meant they disintegrated
with the slightest touch. It was best to eat them quickly

so that your mouth got to enjoy the crumbling,
dissolving sensation and not your fingers.)

BIRTHDAY CAKE
(A butterless sponge; light and fluffy, it was filled
with cream and strawberry jam, and the thinnest
layer of melted chocolate on top. Candles
for the birthday boy or girl.)

TEA-TIME EXPRESS CAKE
(An optional extra, depending on how many
adults were present.)

FANCY BISCUITS
(A large plate of Viscount biscuits in lush green and
orange foil wrappers; Garibaldi biscuits snapped into
uneven pieces; any one of the Kimberly, Mikado and
Coconut Cream trio; and Bourbon Creams.)

CHOCOLATE RICE KRISPIE BUNS
(Mandatory at every party.)

We couldn't start the sweet course until the birthday
rituals had been played out. Mum lit the candles and
whoever was nearest the switch turned out the lights. Kevin
blew out the candles, we clapped and sang an awkward
'Happy Birthday' and 'For He's a Jolly Good Fellow' – no one
made eye contact throughout – and then it was almost time
to cut the cake.

Before this could be done, there was one final ritual to be
endured – it fell to the birthday boy or girl to make a speech.

Everyone had to be thanked for 'coming to my party' and 'for all the lovely presents'. No matter how embarrassing it was or how near tears I felt when it was my party, with a heat rash breaking out in blotches on my neck, I'd have to stand up and give the 'minimum requirement' speech. Trembling and hot, it would take me a few minutes to calm down afterwards. There could be quite a wait for cake on Catherine's birthday. Enjoying the limelight from an early age, she always gave a full speech at her parties, with some funny ad-libs too. Kevin and Lucy, however, were worse than me. Both had been known to burst into tears and bolt from the room or crawl under the kitchen table when it was their turn to make the speech. This year was no exception. Kevin started to blush and ran from the room before uttering a word of thanks. Without Dad to chase up the stairs after him and drag him back, it fell to Grandma to fetch him. Back in the kitchen, we pretended not to hear her gently cajoling and humouring him. He reluctantly returned and muttered the briefest and most ungracious speech. Then at last Mum cut the cake.

I spent the rest of the evening moaning and rubbing my stomach. It seemed to have stretched and swollen to several times its natural size. I loosened my skirt at the side and pulled it down a little so that not even the slightest contact was made between the band and my waist. I couldn't draw attention to my discomfort, as that only brought with it a scolding and a lecture from Mum about greed, and greed being a sin. Instead, I kept my moaning and belching as discreet as possible and suffered in silence until bedtime.

Delia

Few television programmes got my mother's attention. *Dallas*, *Roots* and *The Late Late Show* were the exceptions. For *Dallas* and *Roots*, I was sent to bed for a reason unknown to me, though I was sure it had something to do with adults in bed with sheets wrapped tightly across their bare chests. I was never allowed in the room when programmes like that were on. For *The Late Late Show* I was also in bed but that was because it was on too late and far too boring for me to watch. On Mum's television nights, she washed up quickly after dinner. I watched her fill the copper kettle, prepare her mug with coffee granules, and set two biscuits on a saucer. Then, before she poured the hot water, she sent Kevin and me to our beds. From upstairs, I heard her pull out the pouf from its corner and sit down to watch the week's instalment.

Delia Smith's Cookery Course led to another such night. It wasn't an exciting drama and it wasn't Gay Byrne, but we regarded it as a right of sorts for Mum to watch it – that's what mammies did.

'It's nearly time – you can turn it over now,' she'd call into the sitting room on Delia nights. Begrudgingly one of us would slope over to the television and see the last of *The Incredible Hulk*, *The Six Million Dollar Man* or *Wonder*

Woman as the dial was turned to the BBC. Mum would hurry into the sitting room when she heard the opening credits, with her supper in one hand and a few scraps of paper and a Biro in the other. Catherine, Lucy and Kevin would make their annoyance clear as they filed out of the room, and for half an hour Mum would scribble furiously in her Pitman shorthand. She'd pause now and then to watch Delia layer potatoes and vegetables in a casserole or stuff cannelloni with a piping bag. She'd nod at the screen in understanding and then scribble her notes again.

I stayed to watch Delia, as I liked the way her freckly hands moved about her airy and tidy kitchen. Her hands were sensible and hard-working hands, too, like my mother's. They made every task look simple. I wanted to be like Delia when I grew up. I wanted to stand still in a kitchen and put tiny bowls of ingredients into bigger bowls and shove all the dirty, empty dishes aside for someone else to clean. It seemed glamorous to be cooking without all the mess and preparation work – to be doing the glory work and getting all the *oohs* and *ahs*, without having to weigh, chop, peel, grate, mince, grind and, worst of all, wash up.

Some of the recipes Mum tried straightaway. And they worked. 'I swear by Delia!' she'd gasp upon receiving praise for her latest creation. If she neglected to try a recipe within a week or two, the scrap of paper got buried under the next week's notes and then the following week's notes, never to be seen or tasted. Eventually when Mum tidied out her recipe drawer, unable to make out her own shorthand, she'd fling most of the recipes in the bin. Only a few would survive the cull.

Watching Delia every week mattered less now, as Dad had given Mum the first volume of Delia's *Complete Cookery Course* for Christmas. Or, as I suspected was the case, Mum bought it for herself and wrapped it up for Dad to give to her in front of us on Christmas morning. There was something in the way she said, 'Oh thanks, Tom, it's a book. I-HOPE-IT'S-DELIA'S-BOOK-IS-IT?' that suggested Mum was prompting, rather than thanking, him. She put on a good show of surprise and pleasure at receiving the book and thumbed through it as though she had never laid eyes on it before. It was a dense tome, with hundreds of straightforward recipes but only a few pictures. However, its instructions were clear and the recipes required what Mum described as 'normal' ingredients – Dunnes Stores and Quinnsworth stocked them. I loved to sit at the kitchen table on dreary afternoons and read this book, along with the more colourful cookery books in Mum's collection. I flicked to the picture pages and imagined what Creole Chops, Cheese Potatoes, Shoo-Fly Pie or Crêpes Suzette tasted like. I did my best to persuade Mum to make them.

So over time Mum's urgency to keep up with Delia's programme waned, and we hogged the television until bedtime with few interruptions. Once in a while she did pull rank and request a channel change to Delia. But I didn't mind. I stayed with Mum and watched as Delia took 'one I prepared earlier' out of the oven. I wondered what happened to the other three dinners she had to make, in order to show us the various steps it took to make just one. Did she freeze them? Give them away to poor people? Let the cameraman take them home to his family for tea? There was lots to think about when Delia was on television.

A Marathon

I kept my five pence pocket-money in a red metal tin shaped like a treasure chest. It had a slit at the top to put the money in and a rubber stopper on the bottom to let it out. On weekends I was allowed take a few pennies from the tin and walk as far as the corner shop with Kevin to spend some of it. I'd not received any pocket-money since Dad went into hospital and my stash was dwindling. But I was looking for solace. I wanted some fun. I prised off the rubber stopper with Mum's nail scissors and shook out all the money I had left. Together Kevin and I walked hand in hand and crossed the road carefully. I didn't know the name of the people who ran the shop. I didn't pay attention to the sign above the door or to the elderly woman behind the counter. It was simply the corner shop to me.

The array of penny sweets displayed under the glass counter was thrilling; bright colours, animal shapes, frostings, coatings and dustings. The glass jars, up high on the shelves behind the shopkeeper, were brimful of Black Jacks, Sherbet Pillows, Gob Stoppers, liquorice-filled Bullets, yellow and white dusty Bon Bons, Cola Cubes that cut the roof of your mouth with their sharp granulated coating, and Pear, Apple and Clove Drops. These sweets had to be put on the scales that sat up on the counter, with its long finger pointing out the weight of sweets being measured. This, in turn, was converted to a money amount. I was intimidated by this process of weighing and measuring. Never sure if I'd enough money to pay, I avoided these sweets. There were other sundry items that titillated me and occasionally I spent my money on them: Rice Paper, which was novel but almost tasteless, Liquorice Wraps, Candy Cigarettes with their pale pink burning tips, red candy lipsticks that I ran around my lips before gobbling, soft Milk Teeth that I bared like a childish Dracula, and my favourite, the Sherbet Dip that I could make last the entire walk home.

But for me, treats and escapism were all about chocolate. Chocolate bars were more expensive than sweets and they sat in neat rows in their display case, behind glass and just out of arm's reach. It was difficult to make a choice, as each one meant something different to me. Mentally I established the expected pleasure quotient of each bar, then compared this to all of the others in a complex play-off in my head. This mathematical model had to be processed in a few moments as I stood in front of the shopkeeper, staring hard through the glass. A finger of Fudge was not enough for me, I wanted to feel completely satisfied. A Curly Wurly was long and value for money but it was not gooey enough and most of the chocolate fell off the toffee in little pieces during its stretch, before I got it into my mouth. A Picnic bar was chewy but it did not have a thick chocolate coating; it was just like a Rice Krispie bun with an extra bit of toffee. Bars of Cadbury's Fruit & Nut, Tiffin and Golden Crisp were tempting; I liked the thought of eating the bars my parents preferred and eating all eight squares by myself, but it felt a bit too grown-up for me – they were unlikely to yield any amount of fun.

A Star Bar was close to perfection, having all the necessary ingredients for pleasure – thick chocolate, chewy toffee, peanuts, and it was fun to eat. I ate my Star Bar the same way each time – nibbling away at one side of the toffee the entire length of the bar and folding back what was left of the toffee tunnel, to reveal the peanut roll within. Then I ate this buttery log on its own, before folding all the toffee and chocolate into a ball and shoving it into my mouth, for what resulted in a long dribbly chew. I was resolute, the Star Bar was it. Until my eyes settled on a Mars bar. The chocolate on top was very generous in places, the toffee was of a softer, stretchy consistency that flopped back onto my chin after a big bite and the nougat was the only nougat I ever ate. But a Mars bar did not have the peanuts of a Star Bar.

The decision got harder the longer I stared at the rows and rows of bars, tilting down towards me. And then I saw a Marathon. A Mars bar with *more*. A Mars bar with peanuts – how could I pass it over? Without undertaking a final cross-referencing of the pros and cons of the various options before me, I made my choice – a Marathon, please. I was happy to trade several weeks' pocket-money for the chunkiest, nuttiest and most pleasing chew. I was satisfied with my choice for once.

Slowly we strolled home together. Kevin opened his Sherbet Dip and made exaggerated sucking noises after each dunk. I bit the wrapper off the Marathon bar and chomped straight into it – without having to offer a bite to anyone else first, as was the rule at home. I savoured the thick and cloying sensation of chocolate and toffee as it lodged in the gaps around my teeth and over my tongue and the roof of my mouth. I relished the nut and toffee mix as I churned it around. It only lasted four large bites. As we approached our house, I picked at the nuts stuck in my back teeth and ran my tongue around my mouth to mop up any remaining hint of chocolate on my gums. Having ensured that I'd got to eat the entire bar by myself, I arrived home feeling more than a twinge of guilt for my greed.

Wine

The wonderful pleasure of the chocolate had faded by the time I reached the garage door. It lay open and Kevin and I walked through the garage and into the kitchen to see Mum looking wild and wide-eyed with splashes of deep red across her apron. She was hurriedly mopping at a red puddle on the kitchen floor and around the sink. I panicked. Was Mum sick now too? Where was all this blood coming from?

I turned and saw the large empty glass jars sitting on the garage floor – demijohns, Dad called them. Mum had poured the entire contents of each down the drain. Without Dad around she didn't know what to do with them. She didn't want their constant presence reminding her of Dad, each time she opened the hot press door. Without explaining anything to us, she slumped down at the kitchen table, put her head in her hands and, for the first time, she cried openly. I hesitated and then slowly walked over to her crouched figure and put my arms around her neck. She shook and heaved. She turned into me and we hugged for a very long time.

Dad's experiments with wine had started a few years previously. He'd heard about it from a friend. This was an unusual hobby for a lifelong member of the Pioneer Total Abstinence Association but it was part of his self-sufficiency drive, so he was keeping an open mind. The initial outlay involved purchasing a few large glass jars with oddly shaped stoppers and a few packets and sachets of magic powder. After this investment there would be big savings, he was assured. He could make six bottles of wine for less than the price of one bottle of Blue Nun.

Carefully he followed the instructions. I watched as he poured vast amounts of water into the demijohns and sprinkled in the contents of the sachets. After some stirring and shaking he lifted the heavy glass jars upstairs and placed them inside the hot press, where they remained, tucked in snugly beside the hot tank, for months on end. When I opened the bottom of the hot press, to put in wet shoes or clothes, I stared at the crimson liquid. Sometimes large bubbles filled the neck of the jars. At other times these bubbles went right up into the weird stopper.

As Dad gained confidence in wine-making, Mick, his mentor, decided it was time to forgo the packets and go straight to the source. The elderflower. It was in season during May and June and freely available on roadsides everywhere, he told us. Kevin and I, being too young to have other engagements, were dragged, with large plastic buckets, up the Dublin Mountains. We drove around with Dad and Mick all afternoon stopping at bushes here and there. While Dad passed along the bushes with secateurs, we followed behind him, picked the large branches with white flowers off the ground and filled our containers. We whinged each time the car stopped at a fresh cluster of bushes. We were bored and there was no sign of this task ending. We didn't stop picking until our car was full of elderflowers and the thousand tiny flies we'd inadvertently harvested along with them. We complained all the way home, swatting and flicking at the clouds of these pests hovering around our heads. I felt seriously aggrieved.

We stopped at Mick's house first and handed our haul over to him, as only he had the right equipment and know-how to make the wine straight from the flower. By what means alcohol was extracted from those weed-like bushes was never revealed to Dad. Instead, many months later, we got a few bottles of wine for our trouble. 'Elderflower 1979' was written in Mick's curly hand across the fresh label he had stuck on each bottle. This wine was placed on a shelf in the garage, right beside Dad's own hot-press vintage.

While Mum had the honour of tasting the very first glass from each vintage, she never finished it. Luckily for the visitors to our house, they were never required to do more than admire the row of neatly labelled bottles, lined up on the garage shelf. They were offered a taste, too, but no one ever accepted. They demurred with polite refusals – 'It'd be a shame to open the bottle just for me', 'Sure, keep it for a few years and it will only get better with time'.

Dad's wine was one of the few things I was never that keen to try. While the colour was pretty, its smell was strong and the expression on Mum's face was all I needed to see. With all these bottles at her disposal, she keenly scoured news-papers and magazines for recipes that required wine. Coq au vin, beef bourguignon, chicken with white wine and mushrooms, all started to make regular appearances at our table.

When Mum and I pulled back from our embrace, her eyes

were puffy and red. My nose was running and my face was wet, too. She grabbed a few tissues from a box and we both smiled faintly at each other. We wiped our faces, and finished cleaning up the mess together in silence.

The Recipe Drawer

There were four drawers in our kitchen. The top one held the cutlery, neatly separated in a bright orange plastic organiser. The next drawer down was where Mum kept the clean tea towels – red-and-white check, blue-and-white check and a few souvenir ones featuring the Eiffel Tower or London Bridge – folded neatly and ready for use. The third drawer was called the Junk Drawer, as it held exactly that – a miscellaneous collection of playing cards, tiny toys from inside Christmas crackers, Sellotape, dice, loose elastic bands, throat lozenges, occasional sticks of chewing gum, loose plasters, old balls of Blu-Tack, scraps of paper for note-writing, and lots of grit and crumbs on the bottom that jammed under my fingernails when I shoved my hand in to grab something. The bottom drawer was Mum's Recipe Drawer.

This drawer was crammed full of magazine and newspaper cuttings and recipes written in her own hand, or her sister's or a neighbour's. Anyone who served up a tasty meal, dessert or cake was asked to reveal their secrets to Mum, and these spilled onto the floor when the drawer was opened. Underneath all the loose scraps was Mum's recipe notebook. She received it as a present when she got engaged – her new role very clear – and into it she carefully wrote the recipes for the first food she nervously prepared for her new husband. Gammon steaks with pineapple, brown stew, Madeira cake and Curry cake – recipes neatly written into the first few pages of the notebook; the remaining pages were blank.

While originally only one inch thick at the spine, the book now gaped open to five or six inches. It regularly got so fat with all her inserts that it made closing the drawer impossible. When this happened, Mum sat down at the kitchen table with the contents of the drawer spread out in front of her and attempted to put some order on her collection. Her categories were Meat, Stews, Fish, Pastry, Desserts, Cakes, Tray-bakes, Breads, and Miscellaneous – the last being the largest. Carefully she scanned each scrap and cutting and considered the likelihood of ever making its recipe – honestly. She discarded those that had lain for too long without ever being made. The desserts that involved, not only pastry, but also an egg custard filling, a glaze and gelatine got dumped; they may have originally impressed her with their beauty but she knew she would never get the time to make them. Similarly, dinners that involved a marinade or a sauce on the side got ditched in favour of the one-pot recipes she loved dearly. She kept others that, although well past their use-by date, she considered worthwhile for some unspecified reason – she gave them a stay of execution, with the serious intention of using them … soon. When she could cull no more, she placed the notebook back in the drawer – with a few loose recipes kept apart, as these were frequently used, or were too difficult to categorise. And still the drawer would barely close.

The hoarding resumed unabated. The latest episode of Delia's programme would see at least two fresh recipes added, Saturday's Women's Section in the newspaper provided another, and there were a few from Aunty Mary in England. Each of these took their turn on top of the pile, until they got buried by their successors. Experience showed that if Mum didn't try a recipe straightaway, chances were she never would. Most recipes only saw daylight when the Recipe Drawer refused to close again.

Gadgets

Mum did not get a food processor when they emerged as the 'must have' of the neighbourhood mothers. In other kitchens a big Krups or Moulinex took pride of place on the kitchen countertop, with the lethal-looking attachments just out of reach. But Mum continued to chop, shred, grate, mix, grind, purée, blend, knead and slice by hand. She managed to convince herself that food processors were a waste of time. She assured me that by the time all the bits and pieces were dismantled, washed and put away, she could have done the work faster by hand. Instead, Mum relied on a plethora of less impressive yet novel 'time-saving' devices.

Mum brought home the mandolin from a Saturday morning shopping trip with Grandma in Switzer's. They had been impressed by the in-store demonstration and Grandma insisted on treating Mum to one. Back in our kitchen, I stood at Mum's elbow as she lifted the bright orange slicer out of its box, and with lots of warnings for me not to touch anything, she started to experiment. She brought in the bag of potatoes from the garage and said she was going to show me how to make chips, in a flash! She washed and peeled the potatoes first and then she was ready. She tried a flat blade, then a blade with serrated edges; she even tried slicing the potato first but no matter what she did she couldn't get the chips she had seen during the demonstration. Then she said she'd try shredding cabbage for coleslaw. She cut the cabbage into manageable pieces then quickly slid each piece across the blade. Too thick. She tried a different setting. Still too thick. And so she tried a narrower setting again. Eventually the cabbage fell away into the bowl below in the requisite slices. It was only luck that one of her fingertips didn't join the cabbage.

The mandolin was put to use on a few occasions during its first month in our house – mainly to make coleslaw. As soon as Mum felt she had used it enough to justify its purchase price, it was forgotten about. It lived out the remainder of its life in its original cardboard box, high up on top of the kitchen press, getting sticky with dust and grease.

The electric whisk, on the other hand, was a huge success. I dreaded being asked to beat cream on a Sunday with the hand whisk. It required strength and dexterity I just didn't have. I'd hold the whisk firmly with my left hand, keeping my arm rigid while my right arm rotated the handle around and around and around until my muscles ached. And still the cream was liquid in the bottom of the bowl. I'd have to ask Dad to take over. The electric whisk transformed this task. Now the only challenge was to turn it off at just the right time, to stop the cream turning into butter before my eyes. Mum was never pleased when she had to present a bowl of dry, crumbling and solidified cream with her apple tart.

We got a SodaStream a few years after other people had tired of them. Aunty Mary brought it with her as a present from London. She insisted Mum and Dad would find it saved them lots of money, and with numerous demonstrations, she convinced them it was convenient and easy to use.

Mum took to the SodaStream with enthusiasm. She persuaded herself she was being thrifty by using it. She gave each of us a personal demonstration. I thought it was very futuristic. When it injected gas into a bottle of tap water, it made a psssssst sound, like the opening and closing of the doors on the Death Star in *Star Wars*.

Over the course of its first summer, however, the SodaStream's popularity waned steadily. I liked helping myself to fizzy orange and 'cola'. There was something charming about being self-sufficient when it came to soft drinks. Then it started to dawn on me that our occasional treats of fizzy drinks had now been downgraded. No more Lilt or Cidona – SodaStream didn't do those flavours. We could choose from 'white lemonade', 'orange' or 'cola' – or whichever one was in the supermarket that week. And while Aunty Mary insisted that in a blind-taste test you couldn't tell the difference between SodaStream and real Coke, you could. I could. It was never fizzy enough and definitely not sweet enough. Luckily for me, Mum's enthusiasm also started to wane when she found herself going from shop to shop, doing a ten-mile round trip in search of gas cylinders and concentrate, neither regularly stocked anywhere. Before summer was over the SodaStream was in the corner of the garage, behind bicycles and deck chairs, only to be taken out again when Aunty Mary visited, so as not to hurt her feelings.

The deep fat fryer probably saved our house from incineration. There were several close calls with the big saucepan of hot oil that preceded it. Mum always kept a damp tea towel handy when it was chip day, just in case. There was considerably less drama and tension when chips were being cooked in the deep fat fryer. It did, however, bring its own problems – the nasty job of changing the oil and the filter. Somehow this slipped into the realm of 'men's work', and so Dad begrudgingly took on that task.

The shallow egg poacher, with four saucers suspended over a *bain-marie* of hot water, came from Grandma's house. It almost worked. Unlike poaching an egg in water, when most of the white disappeared into the bubbles, in the poacher the entire egg settled into its tiny bed to be cooked from below. The only problem with our poacher was that it was aluminium, made long before Tefal had invented non-stick cookware. No amount of butter prevented the egg from sticking. While it did manage to preserve all of the white of my egg, I inevitably lost most of the yolk as I scraped and tore the egg free with my knife. Preferring the taste of yolk over white, this was not a good utensil for me.

The cheese-slicer Mum brought into the house a few years earlier worked, but so too did a sharp knife. You placed a block of cheese on a tiled board and brought a thin wire down through it. It cut straight, even slices, it cleaned easily and was used regularly. Then the wire snapped. Known for his ability to fix most things and reluctant to buy a new slicer, Dad took me on a bus into town to Waltons music shop.

Out of his natural habitat, it took Dad a while to find what he was looking for, then he poked around rows of guitar strings until he selected one that looked the right thickness. The boy that served us at the cash register had long hair and a gold stud earring, his jeans were ripped and had big holes at the knees. He was not the type of boy I saw around our roads.

'What kind of guitar is it you have?' he asked Dad, evidently curious as to which one of us was the rocker – the tired middle-aged man in the gabardine or the chubby kid in the bright green coat.

I froze. I knew I was about to be embarrassed by my Dad for the first time and I didn't think I would be able to cope with the ensuing mortification.

Dad replied without guile. 'Oh it's not for a guitar, it's for my cheese-slicer.'

I wanted to be anywhere but there, in my buttoned-up coat with my cheese-eating Dad, in front of that boy who was trying, but failing, to contain his mirth. I know I heard an explosion of laughter as the shop door swung shut behind us. Days later, in the privacy of my bedroom, when I recalled that scene my cheeks still burned red hot. And every time I sliced cheese with the slicer, with the B string taut in its handle, I blushed with embarrassment.

Mum had a range of small utensils that she was very proud of. Her apple corer, which with enough wrist strength and control was useful to have to hand for the occasional baked apple. The 'Parisienne spoon', or butter-baller, as it was known in our house, made posh spheres of butter or melon to impress on special occasions. The hand-held electric blender made a sauce that had gone lumpy silky smooth in seconds. The pressure cooker made tender and tasty stews in no time out of cheap cuts of meat. The small, wooden-handled, corn-on-the-cob holders looked good in their special holder; they were never used. The metal half-moon-shaped lemon squeezer, which enabled a diner to squeeze a half slice of lemon over their dinner with considerably more mess than if they'd done it by hand, was always put on the table but rarely used by those of us in the know.

Some gadgets were too complicated and had too many bits to be thought of as time-saving. Others failed to live up to their promise. Only a few stood the test of time.

Tea-Time Express

Dad was getting out of hospital. I couldn't wait. I'd been good all morning. I even tidied my bedroom without being asked. I put on my best dress and tights and my good winter coat. We went with Mum to pick him up, all four of us sitting on the back seat, keeping the front passenger seat free for Dad. The atmosphere in the car was uniform – everyone was giddy. I was excited to be seeing Dad again. I wondered if he'd look different or act different.

I'd never been in a hospital before. Its noxious smell wafted into my face when we stepped inside the main door. It clung to my hair and clothes and followed me up many flights of stairs. It filled my nostrils and wouldn't go away. I was too hot and the wool of my coat made my neck itch. I stared hard into each room as Mum marched us through long corridors, now familiar to her, and past nurses' stations. I stared intently at everyone. I wanted to be the first to lay eyes on him. I wanted to be the one to shout out 'There he is!' and run into his arms. There were people everywhere, propped up in beds, lying under thin covers, shuffling about in pyjamas, sitting in dressing gowns in communal TV rooms. It was awful. It was so big and so full of sick people, I want to run away from it. How could we have left Dad in such a place, all alone, for so long?

And then I saw him, sitting on the edge of his bed, his small tartan bag closed on the floor by his feet. He was staring straight ahead until he heard ten feet clattering in his direction. He looked around tentatively. Was he afraid to see us? Or was he afraid that it wasn't us at all, but some other rowdy family here to collect a loved one? There was a split second of hesitation before each of us leaned in for a hug. He was smaller but he was Dad. I kissed his pale cheek. I didn't have to be told to be gentle. Dad's thin frame and gaunt face signalled the need for tenderness. The bandages around his neck and the pink dye on his skin held my attention all the way down stairs and back to the car.

A Tea-Time Express was a big deal in our house. Even though any cake Mum ever made was lighter, fresher and more substantial, a 'Tea-Time' – as we called it – was a treat. It was usually when there was a family gathering – Grandma's birthday, a visitor from abroad, or a Christmas get-together – that one appeared. A thoughtful, slightly more affluent relative might arrive at our house and proudly present Mum with the fancy red box with a yellow ribbon tied round it. 'Oh you shouldn't have!' Mum would say. 'Thank you very much. I just love a Tea-Time!' And she'd take it from them and place it squarely on her kitchen countertop. The Tea-Time Express was so exclusive it couldn't be bought just anywhere. Only some shops sold it. There was even a whole shop just for Tea-Time cakes in Dawson Street. Very occasionally Mum brought one home on a Saturday, after her morning shopping in town.

Dad's homecoming was definitely an occasion that needed to be marked with a special treat, so one of Mum's flans or coffee cakes would not do. Mum seated Dad on the sofa in the sitting room, lifted his legs onto the pouf and then returned to the kitchen to prepare the tea and cake.

The Tea-Time was still in its red box, and when it was time to unwrap and cut it, I hovered close to Mum. I loved the ceremony of untying the ribbon (to save it for some other use), lifting the lid on the box, and catching my first glimpse of the cake. My favourite bit was when Mum removed the cake from the clear plastic wrapper and left this aside. As she cut the cake, I scraped my finger along the inside of the wrapper and scooped up any icing and crumbs that were left behind. Some icing yielded better results than others. The fondant icing, for example, stuck to the wrapper in large chunks that my greedy finger scraped up before Mum got a chance to retrieve them and place them back on the cake. If there was a big gathering in the sitting room, Mum would slice the whole cake, and carefully place the overlapping portions on a fancy doilied plate.

There was Strawberry Layer and the more exotic Pineapple Layer. But when the Australian Layer arrived, it immediately became the star of the range. Mum only ever put one layer into her own cakes. Four or five layers, interspersed with jam and the sweetest butter-cream, meant that a slice of Australian Layer melted easily on your tongue. There was even icing on the sides, so every portion was generously endowed. No one wanted the heel or the crust of other cakes – they were too dry and hard. With the Tea-Time, there was a fight for the last outer piece. The excess icing had oozed and lodged here during the cutting, and sometimes there was even more icing than cake in this last slice.

When all was ready, we joined Dad in the sitting room and Mum passed around cups of tea, glasses of milk and slices of delicious Australian Layer. I listened attentively as Dad told us of his stay in hospital. Unused to the spotlight, he was not forthcoming enough for my liking – he needed to tell the minor details that make up a good story. Mum interjected constantly with titbits about how nice the nurses were, how good the food was, and how Mr McConvey, a very busy man, gave Dad positive news on his last rounds. I tried to stay focused but my eyes were drawn to the last slice of the Tea-Time cake. I was willing everyone else to forget about it.

After an excruciating amount of time, Mum said Dad look tired and needed to be left alone to rest. She tidied everything onto her trolley and wheeled it back into the kitchen. Then, in my usual helpful way, I offered to clean up the dishes so that Mum could return to the sitting room and relax with Dad. Gratefully, Mum accepted my offer. Catherine and Lucy were delighted to be relieved of any cleaning duties and Kevin was happy to play with his toys.

As soon as the sitting-room door was shut and I had the kitchen to myself, I pounced on my haul. In two large bites it was in. But it did not taste as good as I'd anticipated. I licked my fingers to make sure I had not missed the taste in my haste to eat it. I'd eaten too much already. The sugar in the wedge of icing overrode any flavour from the sponge and jam. And thanks to my deviousness, I had a sinkful of dirty cups and plates to wash.

Limits

Mum called us in to dinner. She called us again, her tone a little angry now. Then she yelled for us to come at once. We sat down to a plate of baked pork chop with a thick rind of shiny gristle all along its back, a crisp-skinned baked potato and a pool of peas. On a side plate in front of Mum sat one large but anaemic-looking biscuit. It resembled two pale, giant-sized Rich Tea biscuits stuck together with an orange-coloured filling, visible through the large holes in the top.

'What's that?' I asked.

'My dinner.'

'What is it?'

'It's a Limit,' she sighed.

'Is that all you're having?'

'Yes.'

'Why?' I was really at a loss.

'Because I want to lose a little weight.'

Silence from me. I was digesting this last comment. Is that why Mum sometimes ate smaller potions, or had a yogurt while we ate all the rice pudding, or had crackers when we had sandwiches?

'Can I have them when I'm bigger?' I asked.

This time the silence was from Mum.

Even though Dad was in bed most of the time, there was

a note of optimism in the air. Mum was in need of a fresh start and a diet was her way of achieving this. Each evening I ogled her paltry biscuit. I wanted to try one so badly it might as well have been a Star Bar staring up at me from her plate. Then after a few days, it stopped. The Limits disappeared. I said nothing when I noticed Mum eating the same dinner as the rest of us.

A week passed and I forgot completely about Limits. Then one cold evening, as we sat down to a comforting shepherd's pie, Mum put a plate of dry lettuce and tomato with a white, skinless breast of chicken, curled up at the edges, in front of herself. I asked if she wanted to lose weight again and she said she was on the Scarsdale Diet. When we forked our way through a cheesy, creamy fish pie, she ate an insipid and watery piece of poached plaice. When we ate beef of any kind, she filled up on what Dad dismissed as 'rabbit food'. When we ate pork, she ate more skinless and anaemic chicken breasts.

A while later it was the turn of Unislim. The group met in my school on Tuesday nights. I wasn't happy that Mum was in my school every week and walked down the corridors I'd vacated only a few hours earlier. Some of my pictures and projects were on the walls she passed. I worried that one of my teachers might be working late and see my Mum and talk to her. Teachers' friendly after-hours chats weren't to be trusted. It was always safer to keep parents and teachers apart.

A little Unislim booklet sat on the kitchen countertop, with Mum's meals for the next seven days all listed in great detail. I read it just to make sure that Mum wasn't getting anything nicer than I might be served. There were lots of grapefruit, dusty rye crackers and salad on the Unislim menu. I was never envious of those meals. Limits were a different matter – I wanted to make sure that that never happened again.

Mum changed her clothes before going to Unislim meetings. She put on pale blue cotton trousers, wore flimsy plimsolls, and took off most of her jewellery. The second night she came home from Unislim she was in high spirits. She had lost three pounds. She said she thought her trousers felt a little looser. In celebration she made herself a cup of coffee and stuck two proper Rich Tea biscuits together with a thick chunk of cold butter. She put this little 'sandwich' and one of her chewy flapjacks on a plate and devoured them in front of the television while she watched the news.

A Heart Foundation Diet was next. I overheard Aunty Eileen tell her that it was for very fat people, to help them shed pounds quickly before a lifesaving heart operation. Eileen had given it a go, but she looked the same to me. She handed over a contraband photocopy to Mum; it had been copied and recopied and passed down through a long line of hopeful, serial dieters; it was so faded that it was barely legible. There was lots of ice cream on this plan, which seemed very odd to me, along with cracker breads, beetroot and more white fish. I wanted to go on any diet that said I could eat a large slice of ice cream each evening, but I was not allowed. Mum put on three pounds after sticking to this diet for a few days – she threw it in the bin.

Then Mum tried WeightWatchers. The weekly meetings were in Kevin's school this time and the booklets listed similar foods as those in the Unislim menus. Diets soon blended into each other, one following hot on the heels of another; a life lived by the scales. Grandma grumbled when she visited our house with a greaseproof parcel of her delicate florentines, moist tea-brack or decadent almond fingers and Mum refused to be tempted.

'You're not on a diet again are you?' she said, exasperated. 'In my day you were told you could have "a little bit of everything" and it worked for me. All this diet nonsense – sure, you don't need it anyway!' She was frustrated with her youngest but her voice was tender.

Depending on her resolve that day, Mum relented or not as the case may be. Mostly Grandma drank her tea and ate her cake, while her daughter sipped despondently at black coffee.

Irel Coffee

Dad had not returned to work, so when I came home from school I never knew if he was going to be asleep in the sitting room or in bed upstairs. In order to fatten him up and rebuild his strength, Mum encouraged him to have an afternoon coffee and some cake. Dad did not, as a rule, eat between meals; three square meals a day had long been his dietary requirement. But Mum wanted more flesh on his bones. She asked me to make Dad an afternoon coffee, butter a scone and bring it in to him where he lay asleep on the couch.

The fine granules of Maxwell House or Nescafé was what Mum drank, black. The only way to get coffee into Dad was to give him Irel coffee. Dark and syrupy, it was in a tall narrow bottle that had sticky trickles down the sides. The top was difficult to screw off because years of old sticky coffee had lodged in the grooves. I knew how to make it just the way Dad liked. I placed one spoonful of coffee and two of sugar in a mug, poured in a generous amount of cold milk and stirred it to a grainy paste; then hot water from the kettle was poured in by Mum. I stirred this again until the paste was fully dissolved. Next, I slit open a scone and scraped a fine layer of butter across each open surface, also the way Dad liked. I put the scone and the mug onto a plate and went to the sitting room to waken him. It took a few calls of his name to stir him, then he shuffled himself back up to a sitting position on the couch, reached out for the plate and said thanks. He ate what he was given, without questioning if he wanted it or not, or if he was hungry or not. He was very passive. After a few mouthfuls, he placed his mug and plate on the coffee table, his snack gone, his appetite returning.

The only other use for Irel coffee was as an ingredient in Mum's magnificent coffee cake. Coffee cake was her signature cake, the one she proudly brought to other people's houses, the cake that never failed to please. A tablespoon of Irel in both the cake mixture and the butter-cream icing was all it took to impart the essence of coffee. Mum baked two coffee sponges and stuck them together with a generous amount of her filling. Then she scraped gently at the sides of the cake, to get a pile of crumbs on the countertop. After icing the sides, she up-ended the cake and rolled it like a wheel in the crumbs. Finally she iced the top. The finishing touch, which I was allowed do, was to place seven walnut halves on top; six in a circle around the edge and one in the centre. It almost looked like a shop-bought cake created by a professional. At nine years of age, I was forbidden to drink coffee, so I savoured the illicit flavour in Mum's best cake of all.

Trifle

Dad's homecoming brought with it the return of the weekly roast, which was greeted with unspoken relief and joy by everyone. The last roast we had eaten was the one Grandma had made, with carrot rounds and pale potatoes. I could again take huge pleasure in the dubious sight of a chicken defrosting by the embers of our open fire, or in a joint of beef oozing a pool of deep red blood as it sat in our fridge, thawed and waiting to be roasted. The return of the roast also meant the return of Sunday dessert.

Cheesecake – lemon or strawberry – was a dessert Mum made regularly for Sunday dinner. Bowls were spread out across the countertop: egg whites in one, unused yolks in another, cream in a third, cream cheese in a fourth and gelatine dissolving in the fifth; or if it wasn't a posh recipe, this last bowl would have a packet of Bird's jelly dissolving in it. There was lots of spoon- and bowl-licking to be had when cheesecake was being made. My job was to put twelve digestive biscuits into a plastic bag and bash them with a rolling pin. When Kevin got involved in biscuit-bashing, it was double the fun, with both of us crushing and mushing the digestives, but the amount of sneaky biscuit pieces I could eat, without Mum noticing, was halved.

Unfortunately, however, Mum's cheesecakes couldn't be

relied upon. They were often not worth all the whipping, mixing, dissolving, stirring and bashing. Some were so rubbery as to require chewing before swallowing. Others were watery and full of large air holes and tasted of nothing. Trifle was a much safer bet – always popular and always demolished completely.

Trifle was the only thing Lucy ever made. It was *her thing* in the kitchen. No one else was allowed to make it. It took her the *entire* weekend to prepare her trifle. She started it after her hockey match on Saturday morning and only finished it seconds before dinner on Sunday.

Firstly, she sliced the Gateaux Swiss Roll and neatly lined the bottom of a large glass bowl with it. She then strained a tin of fruit salad through a sieve and poured some of the juice over the sponge. She kept aside the pale cubes of fruit for later. Next she dissolved a packet of Bird's jelly in boiling water and when all the sticky cubes had shrunk and disappeared, she dribbled some of this over the sponge too until it was soggy and pink. The remainder of the jelly she put in the fridge to *almost* set. The key was to ensure that the jelly never set completely at this stage. She had to catch it at just the right time, so it was soft enough to tip onto the sponge and form a distinct jelly layer.

The problem arose when Lucy went outside with Catherine to play with their pogo-stick and forgot about her trifle. When she returned, she charged into the kitchen, opened the fridge and screeched when she saw her deep red and rigid jelly. 'Mu-um, what'll I do?' she whined. Patiently Mum got out a saucepan, filled it with boiling water and placed the bowl of jelly on top. It had to be re-melted and re-set. By Saturday night the jelly was as it should be and ready to be placed onto the sponge and the fruit squashed down into it. This was returned to the fridge. Now it could set to its heart's content.

After Mass and our visit to Grandma's on Sunday morning, Lucy made the custard. She had to make a strong yellow custard, if it was to be thick enough. Bird's Custard Powder was generously added to warm milk and stirred, bubbling, to thicken. It remained in the saucepan, cooling for most of the afternoon, before Lucy gently tipped it on top of the jelly in another even layer. Back again into the fridge it went to set.

As Mum banged around the steaming kitchen that evening, stirring the gravy and draining the vegetables, Lucy sauntered in to finish her creation. There was no room on the countertop for Lucy to plug in the electric whisk, so with minutes to spare she set about manually whisking the fresh cream. The pace of her whisking soon slowed down. She took a break and shook her tired arm and then gave it another go. Eventually she looked over her shoulder, pleadingly, at Mum. If she was frustrated at this untimely request for assistance, Mum didn't show it. She stopped what she was doing and took the whisk from Lucy. Her arm rotated rapidly and the balloons of the whisk became a blur in the thickening cream. Within seconds it was in soft peaks. Lucy spread this on top of the trifle, right up to the rim of the bowl. If there was a block of cooking chocolate in the kitchen, she grated a generous amount of it on top, with a confident flourish. She had made dessert. The bowls, whisk and grater she left in a pile by the sink.

Trifle was high on my list of all-time-favourite desserts. I was banned from making it, so I devoted myself to eating it. I looked through the clear glass bowl at her magnificent creation, and the clean lines of Lucy's layers were impressive. Four distinct and colourful layers, to be enjoyed both individually and as a combination. Eating trifle was a special pleasure, too. Moist and yet crumbly on the bottom, cold and sweet in the middle, topped off with at least an inch of custard and cream and a grating of chocolate. Excitedly I asked for hush at the table, as Mum's large serving spoon entered the trifle. I wanted to hear the farting, sucking noise when the first spoonful was pulled out. It was seldom I got to hear my food making such atavistic sounds.

The fun went out of trifle when Mum discovered a new way to make it. It was supposedly more sophisticated – 'This is the way they're doing it now,' Mum told me – and it didn't take two days to make. Mum tossed the sponge, fresh raspberries and bananas together and poured a real and very pale egg custard over them and let it set with lumps and bumps sticking out haphazardly. She plopped cream in a casual fashion on top. Finally she sprinkled on toasted flaked almonds – cooking chocolate or Cadbury's Flake would no longer suffice. Gone forever were Lucy's clean smooth lines and distinct layers. Why did they have to mess with trifle?

Milk Pudding

There were few things as comforting to me as warm milk puddings, and there were plenty of these to choose from on damp winter nights in our house. Each one brought great satisfaction and a fight over who got the 'scrape' – the overcooked bits stuck to the side of the dish. Mum regularly rotated the puddings in her repertoire to avoid repetition and boredom.

Sago: Clear, softened beads like frogspawn suspended in a white stretchy goo that clung greedily to the side of my bowl. I could only get all the sago off my spoon with vigorous licking and sucking and eventually by resorting to my teeth.

Semolina: Very fine grains whose sole purpose seemed to be to change milk from a white liquid into a pale yellow solid. A large amount of sugar added greatly to the enjoyment.

Rice Pudding: The king of milk puddings. When this was placed in the centre of the table, we fought for the brown skin that formed on top during its baking. Mum cooked it to perfection so that the grains were still intact, with a bit of bite. The creaminess made winter nights endurable.

Farola: While its name suggested something exotic, or at least foreign, this was almost indistinguishable from semolina, except that Mum served this baked pudding with a blob of raspberry jam or some tinned peaches in their syrup resting on top.

Custard: One word – Bird's. Bright yellow and very sweet, it could be poured over anything and paraded as a dessert. I loved it over apple purée, warm prunes, fairy cakes or just on its own. Mum had a unique twist on custard – she put chopped bananas and pears into the thick mixture, then put whipped egg white on top and baked it in the oven until the custard was set and the meringue was golden and crispy.

Blancmange: With the exception of Bird's Custard Powder, this was the only 'packet' dessert Mum ever made. She looked down her nose at Angel Delight and refused, despite my pleading, to put it in her shopping trolley. But for some reason, known only to herself, she thought shop-bought blancmange was acceptable. The raspberry-, strawberry- or vanilla-flavoured powder was stirred into milk and poured into a jelly mould to set. But Mum's blancmange never set. When she lifted the mould off, after hours in the fridge, the dessert would invariably collapse and slither over the serving plate and drip onto the table. This annoyed her but didn't bother us. The Day-Glo pink or shocking yellow provided enough novelty and excitement; we were delighted to be eating hues not found in nature. Mum and Dad never ate it; even Dad with his sweet tooth drew the line at blancmange. The four of us would devour large servings of it in seconds.

Bread and Butter Pudding: Lots of stale bread was required to make this pudding. Bread rarely lingered around long enough to go stale in our house, so we didn't get it too often. From time to time, though, Mum purposefully spread bread out on the countertop for half a day, then she buttered it, layered it with sugar, spices and raisins and poured a mixture of milk and beaten eggs over it before baking it. For a milk pudding, this was too dry for my liking. I was glad we didn't have it too often.

Queen of Puddings: Its name alone suggests that this pudding is a cut above. Breadcrumbs soaked with warm sweetened milk, then topped with raspberry jam and a crown of crispy meringue. The wonderful combination of crunchy sweet meringue and raspberry jam with the soft, slightly savoury taste of the breadcrumbs made this a family favourite. Unfortunately for me, however, this dessert became known as 'Catherine's favourite', and it was always Catherine who got the scrape. On queen of pudding days, she momentarily forgot her sulky teenage angst and with an imperceptible and totally maddening smile, she dragged the empty pudding dish in front of herself and happily scraped away at all the crunchy brown bits of baked jam and meringue, like the big child that she was.

And what was my favourite? I didn't have one. I loved all things milky and sweet and so was in with a chance for every scrape, but I never got priority on any one in particular. I could only look on in envy as Catherine devoured hers.

Milk puddings played a central role in helping Dad get his strength back. Little else seemed to whet his appetite. He was out of hospital a long time now but had to go back in every once in a while for some treatment. He slept a lot and only ate a little. He sat at the dinner table with us, but usually ate Weetabix, soup, or some other bowl food.

Milk puddings, however, held Dad at the dinner table longer than usual. So in the constant struggle to keep him eating, Mum let me make rice pudding for him. She showed me how to rinse the grains in a sieve under running water until the water ran clear. Then I spilled these into a baking dish and sprinkled two tablespoons of sugar over them. Carefully Mum let me pour enough cold milk into her measuring jug to cover the rice. Finally I dropped a knob of butter into the centre of the milk, where it promptly sank to the bottom. I was allowed to lift the dish into the hot oven, with Mum hovering at my elbow.

I beamed as Mum placed the rice pudding in the centre of the table after dinner, a stack of bowls and spoons in front of her. It had a deep golden skin stretched taut across it. The skin was aching to be ripped off and gobbled – normally I would have attempted it – but this evening I wanted everyone, especially Dad, to sit and stare at my simple but perfect creation.

'Sheila made the rice pudding this evening, Tom. Will you have some?' Mum asked ceremoniously, yet unnecessarily, as he never refused rice pudding. With a large table spoon she cut through the skin into the ivory milk-and-beads mixture below.

'I don't feel like it tonight. I think I'll just go inside and lie down,' he said, as he lifted himself off his chair.

I watched his back as he left the room. It was narrow even when wrapped in his thick maroon dressing gown. The sight of his alabaster and hairless ankles shunting across the kitchen in his navy slippers made him look impossibly vulnerable.

I was crestfallen. I didn't want Dad to see just how important this was for me. Why had I placed so much importance on a rice pudding? I was being silly. But it *was* important. I believed that somehow it was vital that he eat my rice pudding.

'Just a small bit?' Mum suggested to his departing back.

'Not now,' he said, with his hand on the door handle. And he was gone.

'This looks lovely,' Mum said brightly, turning to me, choosing to gloss over my obvious disappointment. She couldn't address every single nuance and upset that arose each day – there were too many for her to deal with alone. She kept her head down and divided the pudding into four generous portions – she herself always passed over dessert on week nights.

Taking my lead from her, I said nothing. I ate my dessert in silence. It should have been delicious. I couldn't taste it for the tears rolling down my face.

The Vegetable Patch

It went against the grain with my parents to pay someone for work that could be done in-house. Tradesmen were a rare sight, as Dad used to do all repairs himself. But these days, without his strength and skills around the house, Mum had to rely on herself or employ help. She winced when she wrote a cheque for the plumber who came and bled our radiators – she didn't tell Dad about it. Nor did she mention the few pennies she sponsored our next-door neighbour's Boy Scouts Club for mowing the back and front gardens. She decided, too, that the vegetable garden Dad and she had tended for several years had to go. She couldn't manage it alone – us children were of no help at all. Reluctantly she paid two teenage boys from up the road to turn the soil in our back garden and put an end to their days of suburban farming. It didn't seem right, but she said she had no choice.

Their plan on how to live independently and not rely so completely on commercial enterprises had required Dad to dig up half the back garden and plant rows and rows of round lettuce, onions and peas every year. I knew spring had arrived when I walked into the garage and Dad was crouched over trays filled with compost. He placed tiny seeds precisely half an inch apart and let me press them under the soil with my small fingers. Then these trays were laid out on the kitchen windowsill, watered and tended every evening until seedlings appeared above the surface and grew in strength. When the time was judged to be right, and no more frost was likely, seedlings were planted out in the vegetable patch, and the tender young tomato plants moved to the protection of the garden shed. Planting out was a tedious chore, I always thought. All I ever had to do was the watering and weeding, and only then if I was overheard complaining of having nothing to do.

When the onions were pulled from the ground in early summer, they had to dry out. The stalks had to wither and the protective brown skin had to take hold. Freshly picked onions were lined up on every windowsill that faced the sun. They were placed on trays in the garden under old panes of glass leaning against the wall. They covered any clutter-free surface in the shed for the few weeks it took until they were ready to eat.

During summer, the lettuce sprouted quickly. And before long they looked like giant green roses with layers of leaves wrapped tightly in concentric circles around the firm heart at the centre. These big lush leaves then loosened out and spread across the vegetable patch until Mum pulled them for dinner or slugs got at them.

The pea harvest was usually disappointing. Not only were peas more time-consuming to grow, as they had to be teased up and tied to thin bamboo sticks, but one meal was all we ever got from a whole bed of plants. Perhaps this was because I was given the task of podding them – more peas made it into my mouth than into the colander.

Tomatoes required the most work. Dad spent long hours

in the shed watering and feeding them; Mum joked that he talked to them. Then our neighbour's trees grew out of control and blocked all the sunlight that had shone through the Perspex roof of the shed. No tomato was going to turn from bright green to a succulent red in a dark and shadowy shed. The hot press came in handy to assist with the final ripening. It was getting increasingly difficult to farm under such circumstances.

Beetroot also frustrated Dad. A whole bed of seedlings yielded only a handful of golf-ball-sized vegetables. After a few seasons of failure, he refused to try them again. 'It's the soil,' he complained. 'Oul' builder's muck, no good for beetroot.' It was sufficient for rhubarb, however. Thick stems with giant, prehistoric leaves sprouted effortlessly from their allotted patch. Herbs also grew easily. Parsley, thyme and chives were the only herbs used in Mum's kitchen and for much of the year she was able to get them from the back garden.

There were obligatory *oohs* and *ahs* at the table when a meal was prepared with our home-grown, organic vegetables. A salad with our own lettuce and tomatoes, a stew with a few onions and herbs, a rhubarb crumble – these were all a source of pride for Mum and Dad.

Neighbours and relatives also benefited from my parents' labour. Any caller to our house was sent home with some bright green and mucky lettuce, a bag of onions or a bunch of rhubarb, depending on what was in season on our plot. Maeve's Dad swapped his pears and plums for our onions and tomatoes in a casual barter that benefited both families.

Mum and Dad enjoyed living 'The Good Life'; it was nice

to be self-sufficient in some small but significant ways, even if it was back-breaking and often tedious work. I suspected that there was a small part of Mum that was glad to see an end to the vegetable garden. After all, when you totted up the hours of labour and the back pain and subtracted all the 'gifts' of vegetables they gave away and the vegetables that rotted or never ripened, it probably didn't save them any money at all.

It may have been guilt or sadness that was in her eyes as she stood staring out our kitchen window watching the boys turning the soil that Dad had fortified for the last few years. They sprinkled the fresh earth liberally with grass seed and our garden returned to its original state.

Pancakes

Why did we only have pancakes once a year? Every year Mum swore she would make them another day and every year we only ever got pancakes on Shrove Tuesday. They were greasy and soggy and absolutely heavenly.

Mum made the batter early in the day and then whisked it throughout the afternoon, when she caught a glimpse of the glupe-filled jug resting in the fridge.

Cooking all the pancakes and keeping them hot, so that each of us could have our fill, was a marathon effort. The four spiral rings of the cooker were all on the go. On the front rings there were two frying pans with melting butter sizzling in each; at the back, two saucepans of water bubbled away with dinner plates acting as lids – these were her improvised *bains-marie*. She poured batter into each frying pan and turned the pancakes carefully with her fish slice – Mum did not believe in flipping pancakes – then lifted them to her hot plates when they were cooked. When five were ready, she served them out to her charges and immediately returned to the cooker, where she continued to cook another batch as we gobbled away.

We'd dabbled in the past with apple sauce, golden syrup and honey as toppings, but there was only one that stood the test of time for us – freshly squeezed lemon juice and a generous sprinkling of caster sugar. Rolled up and sliced into bite-sized pieces, the pancakes soon disappeared and it didn't take us more than a few seconds to have our plates out for more.

Mum worked very fast to keep up with demand. The kitchen filled with grey smoke as the butter on the pans became more burnt with each successive batch. The bubbling water from her *bains-marie* added to the steam and condensation. I was oblivious to any discomfort and worked just as fast to squeeze juice, sprinkle sugar and eat quickly to ensure I got thirds and fourths. If I wasn't going to eat pancakes for another year, I was going to cram in as many as I could today.

When Mum got to sit down, only a few small black pancakes remained wilting on the warm plates. Without asking if anyone wanted any more, she smothered them with sugar and lemon juice and relished her quota. Through bittersweet mouthfuls, she promised me she would definitely make them again – before next Pancake Tuesday. I tried to have faith in her this time.

After-Dinner Cigarette

Some meals ended in a fight, sending each of us from the table in different directions. Others saw us drifting off when we had finished our food, and excused and blessed ourselves. But after a satisfying meal, with no rows and all plates cleaned, Mum and Dad got out their packets of Benson & Hedges.

Sitting beside Mum, I watched closely as she slid the cigarette out of its slim gold box. She leaned forward across the table to Dad's lit match, and holding the cigarette to her lips, she gently touched Dad's hand to steady the flame. She inhaled deeply until her cheeks went hollow, the tip of her cigarette went red and the paper burned back a little. She exhaled long and hard, sending her plume of smoke up to the kitchen ceiling above our heads. Then she relaxed back into her chair, sighed and paused a moment before taking another deep drag, usually the longest drag. These were her few illicit moments of quiet relaxation. She was not expected to talk. We knew not to ask her a question. Stillness. A pause hung in the air just above our table. Into this she directed her smoke. I liked to watch the red tip move back along her cigarette. I sensed her pleasure.

But for Mum and Dad this ritual stopped abruptly on Ash Wednesday, 1980. While I was planning to hoard sweets until Easter – except for St Patrick's Day when I got a special dispensation from the Church because it was a very holy Irish day and I could eat as much of my stash as I wanted – Mum and Dad gave up cigarettes for good.

'They're bad for you,' she explained to me, 'and with Dad and everything ...' She trailed off.

So after dinner, Mum – who had also given up sweets, biscuits, cake and chocolate – struggled to drink a lone cup of coffee. She stood up abruptly and started to clear away the dishes from the table while we were still eating. She made it through to Easter without a single cigarette.

Dad, on the other hand, wrestled with his demons for longer. After dinner he reached for a plain biscuit to dunk into his tea. He nibbled at the soggy bits until the biscuit was gone, but the urge was still with him. I could see it in his fingertips as they tapped the side of his cup and fiddled with his teaspoon. He swallowed what remained of his tea in an audible gulp before reaching into his pocket and pulling out a packet of Polo mints. In haste his fingers scraped and teased open the tightly bound foil and he popped one into his mouth. I was doubtful that such a tiny sweet would help.

Finally he sat down after his dinner one evening and took out a pipe and a pouch of tobacco. Mesmerised, I watched him press brown flakes into the bowl of the pipe and set them alight. He puckered his lips and made funny kissing pouts with his mouth around the stem the pipe. Eventually large plumes of smoke billowed out from him, covering his entire family in a blue haze and filling the kitchen with a new, not unpleasant smell. This was how Dad gave up cigarettes.

Easter Eggs

During Lent, Kevin and I were dragged to early morning Mass before school. Mass was at 7.50 a.m. in our parish, and so, while our neighbours' houses remained in darkness, we were dressed in our uniforms and shunted into the car. We sat through a speedy eighteen-minute Mass and then rushed home to gobble breakfast and get to school on time. Some days we went to evening Mass instead. Throughout Lent we roamed from parish to parish, to churches in the Mount Merrion, Univeristy College Dublin, Booterstown, Kilmacud areas – Mum was fickle when it came to getting Mass, any parish with a convenient time would do.

The evenings Mum forced us to say the rosary at home were the worst. We all stood up from the dinner table – Mum didn't even stop to clear up the dishes, in case any of us escaped – and we were corralled into the sitting room. We knelt down on the floor, a few of us leaning on the couch, the rest against chairs or whatever surface was the right height for praying. Dad was allowed to sit on a chair facing us all; he wasn't strong enough to be getting up and down on his knees. Mum was the only one who knew all the Mysteries, so she introduced each one briefly, and without drawing breath, she started to recite a decade of the rosary.

'Today is Monday so it's a Joyful Mystery – the Virgin

Mary was told she was going to be the mother of Jesus. Our Father who art in Heaven, hallowed be thy name ...'

We mumbled our responses to her prayers. The role of leader then moved around the room, along with barely suppressed sniggering. We four children never discussed it with each other before or after prayers, but it was understood that we should compete to see who could say the 'Fastest Prayer' – who could get through a decade at top speed, while still pronouncing all the words and not bringing the wrath of Mum on our heads.

'HailMarfullgraceLordswitheblestarthoumongwomenble stfruitothywombjeez ...'

On rosary nights I prayed for the phone or the doorbell to interrupt the proceedings. If the phone rang, it was answered – unfortunately only the recipient was excused from rosary and no one ever phoned me. If someone knocked on the door, one lucky person was relieved from praying duty. But if someone called or rang for Mum, it meant an immediate end to prayers for all, as Dad didn't take over her leading role and continue in her absence. He preferred to read his newspaper.

On top of all the extra religiousness of the Lenten period was the requirement that we give up chocolate and sweets for six weeks. This included any biscuit with the tiniest hint of extravagance. (Catherine only had to give up bad language. Mum said it was more important that Catherine, as a teenager, stop saying 'damn' and calling people 'spas' than stop eating chocolate. I wished that was all I had to do.) Each time I did an errand up to a neighbour's or helped Grandma, and got a few sweets, a stick of Twix or a lollipop for my troubles, I said thank you and duly took my goodies home to store in a shoe box that I hid in the back of my wardrobe. I tenderly fingered my growing stash, ran my hands over each item and wet my lips in anticipation of their demise. Half a pack of Munchies for helping Grandma weed her garden; a Club Milk from Mrs Devitt up the road for fetching things to help her bathe her youngest; a Walnut Whip for being good for Mum; and some lesser items such as a Sherbert Dip, a Time Bar, a Wagon Wheel, and a few Refreshers for minor chores.

On Easter Sunday all I wanted to see was shiny purple foil. It didn't matter how big or small the egg – though big was definitely better – or if there was a bag of sweets inside or two bars on the outside. Just as long as the box and the foil around the egg were purple, then it was a proper Easter egg.

What I got from Aunty Maudie was a small egg wrapped in red foil. This egg didn't come in a box, nor was it sitting on an eggcup or any kind of container – it was just an egg, on its own. She got them in the markets on Camden Street, around the corner from her house. The chocolate inside the red foil was a dark brown colour, not the milky brown I was used to. Nor did Maudie's egg make the sharp snapping noise I was anticipating as I broke into the shell. Instead of shards of chocolate breaking clean away from the egg, soft lumps of chocolate peeled away from each other in quiet surrender. Its taste was vile, too. Kevin and I loudly spat the chocolate out into our hands. Mum heard us and told us we were spoilt and ungrateful. We just opened our purple eggs instead – to get rid of the taste of Maudie's one.

I spent Easter Sunday and Monday – and every day that

followed – gorging on chocolate until all my eggs and my entire Lenten stash was finished. I was not like Lucy, who stored her eggs under her bed and ate them gradually, in tiny amounts, over the following months. I made myself sick with chocolate. I shoved piece after piece into my mouth in an attempt to capture some taste that I knew was just beyond my reach, a taste that was hinted at but never lingered on my tongue long enough for me to appreciate adequately. So I ate more and more, intoxicating myself in the quest for some elusive taste. I never got it. And I never stopped searching.

Blake's

We went to Blake's Restaurant in Stillorgan for Lucy's Confirmation. I had been to Bewley's with Mum, for a Coke and a cream bun, as a treat after a visit to the optician, or when Aunty Teresa was up from Cashel, but this was the first time the six of us went to a real restaurant as a family. We'd polished our shoes and were all dressed in our Sunday best. We buttoned up our good coats and stood in the hall while Mum and Dad locked up the house and Dad checked his wallet for the third time. After Mum gave each of us a final appraisal, we squashed into our Opel Kadett, Kevin lying across the three girls' knees in the back seat. It was only a short drive, so he didn't complain too much.

The restaurant was large and circular in shape. The window tables overlooked the large car park and the busy roads outside. The centre of the room had a mixture of tables and booths. Getting a booth was great. Sliding across the bench, I felt American. I was one of Charlie's Angels, laughing in a diner with Bosley after rescuing a kidnap victim from merciless villains. It was the moment just before the camera froze and the credits rolled.

Each table in Blake's had its own salt and pepper shakers, an aluminium napkin holder, and a bowl filled with sachets of tomato sauce, vinegar, mayonnaise and brown sauce. The room was so big it got dark towards the centre. Colourful stained-glass lamp shades hung low around the room yet emitted very little light. The carpets were deep maroon with a yellow-gold leaf pattern. There were several serving stations for the waiters and waitresses at key points in the restaurant, where I could see them chatting as they folded napkins and sorted cutlery. It was very impressive. I couldn't wait to be old enough to get a job there. To walk around the restaurant all busy and important, to look smart in the black-and-white polyester uniform and to know what went on behind the swing doors leading to the noisy kitchen – to have access to the magic going on in there – that must be very exciting.

However, there was a bit of tension at our table as we'd been seated beside one of these work stations. As waitresses energetically polished the cutlery, they flung each gleaming knife and fork into the cutlery container, the awful racket drowning out our conversation. Mum kept talking, her voice straining, getting louder and louder as she tried to ignore the clatter and keep the atmosphere light and airy. Dad got cross and fidgety, half-heartedly looking around, as if seeking someone to complain to – but he held his peace. That would have spoilt the mood completely and so he endured the crashing of steel on steel (with a lot of sighing and tutting) until the waitresses got bored with their own industriousness and moved away.

'Isn't this lovely?' Mum said as we set about reading the menu. She smiled broadly as she looked round the table at each of us, her eyes a camera recording the scene for posterity.

Blake's gave us families just what we wanted – big generous portions of safe, filling and affordable food, either baked, roasted or fried, served on thick, scalding hot plates. The menu was large and laminated, with small white stickers here and there noting a price change. Obviously the dishes on offer never changed.

Egg mayonnaise for the starter – a few leaves of lettuce, a wedge of tomato and a slice of drying cucumber provided a nest for a hard-boiled egg, halved, face down and drowned in thick mayonnaise with a sprinkling of paprika on top. Or melon served as a wedge, with the flesh cut into chunks and placed back on the skin, each alternate piece slightly off to the left and the right making a zigzag pattern, with a glacé cherry pierced by a cocktail stick on top. Minestrone soup came in a stainless steel bowl with some bread on the side. The soup of the day, if it was tomato or potato, came with a blob of whipped cream dissolving into it and perhaps a few chopped chives on top.

There was a large selection for the main course: chicken Maryland, chicken Cordon Bleu, chicken and chips, half a roast chicken, chicken Kiev, mixed grill, plain burgers, cheese and bacon burgers, lasagne, spaghetti bolognese, pizza. There was nothing to disconcert on the menu. No need to question the waitress as to nuances of flavour; no fear of getting too many exotic or unidentifiable spices in your dinner. The buttery, garlicky stink of chicken Kiev was as adventurous as it got.

I wanted value for money at Blake's. I wanted a very full plate to be placed in front of me. If I didn't pick the best dinner to arrive at the table, it would take some of the enjoyment out of the meal for me. So I looked around at the surrounding tables to see what other diners had chosen.

The mixed grill looked like a big hitter – at least ten different items squeezed together on the plate. Sausages: two; rashers: two; white pudding: one; black pudding: one; lamb chop: one, possibly two; all served with a pile of fried mushrooms, half a tomato and a generous portion of chips. This was going to be hard to beat!

But even at my young age, I felt I would be better served by trying something different. Something Mum did not cook at home. This is where chicken Maryland came in. It ticked all the boxes. Your plate was piled high, Mum never served battered fruit with her chicken, *and* it came with chips. A large, golden-crumbed breast of chicken served with a banana fritter *and* a corn fritter, a garnish of lettuce, cucumber and tomato and a messy mound of coleslaw, plus half a plate of chips. Another serious contender.

And then of course there was the temptation to order chicken Kiev, as garlic was an ingredient Mum never ever used in her kitchen and I was curious to try it.

The inner struggle to make the right choice was excruciating. What if I chose the mixed grill and only one rasher and one chop arrived? Then again, what if I chose the chicken Maryland and the corn fritters were very small? That was equally risky.

When the waitress arrived and placed a jug of water on our table, I got panicky. I hoped she would start with Mum and work the long way around the table and get to me last. I needed an extra moment to make my decision and to weigh it up against what everyone else was ordering. I didn't want to be in a situation where I would be envying someone else's dinner. I never knew until I opened my mouth what I was going to order.

The waitress looked at me first with eyebrows raised in expectation and her pen poised over her tiny pad.

'Lasagne for me, please.'

What? Why? Lasagne! You idiot! One bowl of stretchy, cheesy goo and you won't even get chips! What were you thinking? I was annoyed with myself even before the food was served.

I was even more disillusioned when the oval terrine of wall-to-wall, bright orange and bubbling cheese arrived in front of me. As I looked around the table at plates of big fat burgers, fritters and fries, even Dad's half roast chicken, plain as it was, looked better than my sticky lasagne. And I got no chips.

Mum, noticing the disappointment I was incapable of hiding, leaned into me and whispered, 'Mmmm, lasagne, that looks lovely! You can try some of my fish and chips, too, if you like.'

This lifted my spirits a little and distracted me just enough to take my mind off everyone else's meals.

Inevitably, though, I enjoyed the comfort of the piping hot cheese and pasta mix. As I forked my way through my creamy dinner, my mind drifted to dessert. I felt under pressure now to try to make up for my rash choice of main course by picking the very best dessert possible. Now what would I go for? Knickerbocker glory, banana split, apple tart with cream or ice cream, trifle, Black Forest gateau …

Ice-cream Float

'You bitch!' Maeve screeched at the top of her voice.

It was a warm afternoon and the taste of summer was in the air. My days in school were numbered; I had survived another year. Maeve had come to my house to play after school and we were outside in the back garden. We amused ourselves with our dolls; we attempted swing ball and played hopscotch; we doodled with chalk on the ground; we sang ABBA songs, back to back, the way the girls did on television. I imagined I was the blonde one, captivating my imaginary audience with my beauty and the blur of the soft focus lens around my face; but Maeve, I knew, was prettier, so I didn't put up a fight and sang as the dark-haired one instead. I was happy and content having Maeve to myself all afternoon.

And just when I thought life couldn't get any better, Mum walked into the garden, unannounced, carrying a tray of two tall glasses filled to the brim with a bright orange drink, which had a strange foam floating on top.

'Have you ever tried an ice-cream float, Maeve?' asked Mum, setting the glasses down in front of us.

'Never,' Maeve replied, wide-eyed and almost breathless with pleasure.

I'd never received such a treat before either. I was unaware that Mum knew of such strange, exotic-looking drinks.

She told us it was made with Club Orange and had a thick slice of vanilla ice cream frothing inside it. And she gave us each a teaspoon, so that we could eat the ice cream and sip our cloudy orange drink as we liked.

After a few delicious sips, I tried to spoon some ice cream, but it was jammed in the bottom of my glass and my spoon was too short to get at it. I tried tipping my glass to the side and into my mouth but nothing would dislodge the lump of ice cream. Maeve's ice cream, I noticed, was bobbing near the top of her drink, so she was able to sip and eat ice cream at the same time. I felt frustrated. Jealously and greedily, my arm darted across the table before I could control it and my spoon dug into Maeve's drink before she could stop me. In my haste, I spilt much of her drink, though I got a spoonful of ice cream for my trouble. The curse she had heard, but had never before used, burst from her at my betrayal.

'Maeve O'Reilly!' Mum roared through the open kitchen window. 'That language is not allowed in this house. You'll have to go home now, ice-cream float or no ice-cream float!'

It was my fault. I was devastated. My afternoon of tranquillity and treats was ruined.

Mum came out of the kitchen, took the coveted drink away from Maeve and marched her towards the door. I'd managed to get Maeve into trouble with my mum and no doubt with hers, too, and I didn't have the courage to own up and take the blame. I didn't pull at Mum's apron and try to stop her banishing Maeve. Instead, I remained rooted to the spot in the garden while Mum stood at the front door, watching Maeve walk home. Then she shut the door behind her, as if doing so would keep her home free from bad language for ever.

She came out to me in the garden. 'Well, madam. What did you do to her?' she asked.

I was ashamed and embarrassed by my own greed. My very own nature had let me down. Through my tears, I mumbled my guilt.

'I should take that away from you, too, you know,' Mum snapped at me. But she didn't. She just marched back into the kitchen and threw the contents of Maeve's glass down the sink in temper.

I persevered with my ice-cream float, the ice cream melting now and rising to the top of my glass. In between bites and glugs, I wondered if I should call up to Maeve – after I was finished – and apologise, or should I wait until after dinner? Maybe the morning would be better; I might not be so ashamed by then.

Scrambled Eggs

There was no meat consumed in our house on Fridays, ever. This was primarily a religious decision, taken by Mum and observed by us all. The financial and health benefits were not lost on Mum either. The alternatives to meat were limited: fish pie, fish fingers or scrambled eggs.

I dreaded Fridays. If the smell of fish greeted me as I entered the house, things were destined to be bad enough. Fish was too smelly, so it either had to be smothered in a rich cream and cheese sauce to get past my taste buds, or come from a Bird's Eye packet. But if the smell of fish was completely absent from the kitchen, it meant only one thing – scrambled eggs.

Scrambled egg was the only food that revolted me. I hated it with a passion. Lightly boiled or hard-boiled, fried or poached – those were the type of eggs that I enjoyed. I couldn't explain why, as a non-fussy-eat-everything-off-the-plate kind of girl, I was repulsed by scrambled eggs. I moaned and pleaded with Mum as she scraped the beaten eggs away from the sides of the saucepan – 'Anything but scrambled eggs, pleeaase.' But Mum made no exceptions. She didn't prepare different meals to meet the diverse preferences of her family. And so I'd stare miserably at my plate of egg bits, wishing them away. I'd poke and play with the tiny beads of bright yellow rubber until there was nothing I could do but eat them – cold. They were tasteless yet revolting at the same time. Perhaps it was the fleshy, rubbery texture that was so off-putting.

Then Mum went to London. She needed a rest, a break for a few days, and Dad was feeling better. He wasn't back at work but he was on the mend, we were told. She was going to stay with Aunty Mary. After numerous hugs and kisses from the four of us and Dad, we waved her off on her big weekend away and Uncle Pat drove her to the airport.

That Thursday evening saw us all at sea. What were we to do now? Without Mum directing us, organising us and filling the house with activity, we were lost. The house was uncomfortably quiet. In the absence of direction from Dad, Catherine and Lucy climbed the stairs to their lair. For a while, Kevin and I followed him around the house and then, realising he didn't know what to do either, we abandoned him.

But after a few hours, Dad warmed to his role. He opened up and began to relish being the only adult in the house – the man of the house for a change. Kevin and I sat beside him on the couch and with little prompting he told us about his bachelor days – days before Mum. He told us how he'd been able to look after himself, with no woman around, for fourteen whole years before he got married. This seemed highly unlikely to me, as the most I had seen him do in the kitchen was make a pot of tea and a sandwich. Mum even sewed buttons on his shirts and darned his socks. Yet he told us how he lived on his own in flats in Drumcondra and Rathgar. How he ate his dinner every working day in a restaurant on Dame Street. He described it as a huge room heaving with country boys and girls, like himself, each being served three-course meals – soup of the day, followed by meat, vegetables and spuds, and finished off with dessert and tea – all for the sum of four shillings and six pence. This was hardly looking after himself, I thought. It seemed like decadence to me. I certainly couldn't reconcile this picture of Dad – in a restaurant every day! – with the careful, frugal Dad I knew today.

On the first evening of Mum's absence, when he tired of recounting his youth to us, Dad offered to make Kevin and me some scrambled eggs for tea. He was recklessly flouting Mum's written instructions to reheat her shepherd's pie. Emboldened by his new-found authority, he was choosing to disregard the numerous sheets of foolscap paper, covered in Mum's frantic scrawl, that she had left, clearly visible, across the countertop. He was turning his back on her list of dinners for each of the days she was away: shepherd's pie to be reheated for day one; fish fingers for day two; a lasagne to be defrosted and reheated at 180 degrees for forty-five minutes on day three; and on day four, Mum would return just in time to save us from starvation.

I despaired at the idea of scrambled eggs, let alone what Dad's version of them would be, but I didn't want our nice time together on the couch to be ruined by me turning up my nose at his first suggestion. I didn't want to hurt his feelings. So I agreed to scrambled eggs for tea.

Dad neatly cracked eggs into the Pyrex bowl. He added salt and a shake of white pepper (never black, he said), and a splash of milk before beating them well with a fork – no such thing as a whisk in his bachelor pad. Then, as the knuckle of butter melted in the saucepan, he popped two bits of bread into the toaster – just the length of time he needed to scramble his eggs. He tipped the mixture into the sizzling butter and started to stir, showing me how he was slowly lifting cooked egg off the bottom and sides of the saucepan. He didn't take his eyes off the eggs. He watched them closely for changes in colour and texture. Then suddenly, when his experience told him the time was right, and I thought they were still raw and runny, he took the eggs off the heat and stirred vigorously as they continued to cook. Pop! The toast was done. The eggs rested a minute while Dad evenly buttered the toast. Then he placed one slice on each plate and gently spooned the soft and shiny eggs on top.

'There you go!' he said, with a confidence I was sure was undeserved and inappropriate. And he slapped two plates down on the bare table in front of me and Kevin.

'Thanks,' I mumbled with low expectations, as I bravely poised my knife and fork over the eggs.

To my amazement they were like no eggs I had ever tasted before. These scrambled eggs actually tasted of eggs – but nicer. Together with the buttery toast, they were actually divine. The softness of the eggs and the crunchiness of the toast were a perfect match for each other. This was the moment I discovered that scrambled eggs and meatless Fridays did not have to be dreaded and loathed any longer.

Mum came home from London laden with bags of presents. I got a Beefeater doll standing upright in a clear plastic cylinder, and a key ring of miniature postcards of London that all folded up neatly and closed into a tiny, red leather book with the snap of a popper. Each of us got a sleek purple box packed tightly with my favourite small squares of Cadbury's chocolate, individually wrapped.

Mum told us, hour for hour, what she did each day in England – where they shopped, who they met, what they ate – as we each devoured as many of our chocolates as she allowed, before going to bed later than usual that Sunday night. Normality was restored to the house the next morning. Dad was absent from the kitchen, porridge was warming on the cooker and a block of meat was oozing blood, defrosting for dinner that evening.

The Friday after Mum's return there was no fish smell in the house. It was going to be scrambled eggs for tea. The words were out of my mouth before I could stop myself. 'Why can't Dad do the scrambled eggs tonight? His are much nicer!'

This hurt her, I could tell. Perhaps I intended it to. But a comment like this was also liable to open up a can of worms. Mum had been known to 'go on strike' from time to time. When the burden of housework swamped her completely and her ungrateful family failed to notice or compliment her hard work, she occasionally exploded. A misjudged comment was sometimes all it took for Mum to start ranting about all she did, unassisted and unappreciated – hoovering, ironing, cleaning, dusting, washing and more washing, shopping – an endless list of chores would be spewed out. And suitably shamed and apologetic, we'd all promise to help. The five of us would decide – were told – to share the burden of housework, Mum drawing up a rota of duties and sticking it on the fridge. She'd let the washing build up;

she'd refuse to clear the sink; she'd serve brown bread for dinner, as each one of us learned to help with hoovering, cleaning, dusting – for a few days. Then gradually, task by thankless task, Mum would take over again, and before a week was out, everything would be as before.

However, this time, instead of getting wounded or angry, Mum stopped her frenzied egg-stirring and toast-making, placed her hands on her aproned hips and looked hard at me, debating internally how to respond. Her confrontational stare was accompanied with a long sigh. Together they conveyed to me my complete ignorance. Did I not see that there was no chance my dad was going to get up from his supine position in front of the six o'clock news to make scrambled eggs for everyone? I had to learn to live with Mum's version – and not another word was to be said about it.

I was embarrassed by my own stupidity and regretted hurting Mum, so I said nothing else on the matter. It was a long time before I got to taste creamy scrambled eggs again.

Gristle in her Gullet

The most positive sign of Dad's returning health was when he and Mum had their first proper argument in months.

For Mum there was no respite from the hard work that was required of her, and Dad being home from work and needing extra attention added to her burden. The high standards of mothering, imposed largely on her by herself, meant that she was our servant and she never got a break. She was constantly on the look-out to ensure that all five of us were happy, that we wanted for nothing. Mostly she expressed this concern and love through the food she put before us. A small plate of brown bread and jam could be slipped in at my elbow when my head was bent low over a join-the-dots picture. A leftover slice of pavlova could be shared with her to help heal a scratched knee. A slice of spotted dick and a cup of warm milk made the arrival home from school even more welcome. As a result of this overwhelming instinct to nurture and provide through food, Mum dominated completely in the kitchen. Which suited the five of us very well.

This also meant that during mealtimes Mum spent most of the time on her feet. She insisted on washing the saucepans at the same time as serving the dinner. She continued scrubbing at the sink when the rest of us began eating, until we paused, noticing her absence from the table, and Catherine or Dad, as the figures of some authority, insisted she sit down. We'd resume eating when Mum made the first cut into her dinner. Then if Dad asked where the salt was, or if Lucy needed vinegar, or Kevin wanted tomato sauce, Mum would push back her chair and hop to her feet as if an order had been barked out by a drill sergeant. Within seconds the named condiment would appear, the lapse in her foresight amended. She rarely paused to suggest that someone younger, more agile and sitting closer to the fridge or press do the fetching.

On the day of Mum and Dad's argument, Mum was making slow progress with her dinner as usual. She asked each of us children how our day went and she told us about hers. And Dad, even though he didn't have much to tell, was asked for his contribution, too. Mum chaired the mealtime chat.

Dad continued to eat his dinner, and added little to the conversation. This clearly irritated Mum. After too many minutes of paternal silence, she challenged him. He wasn't so sick any more that he couldn't be confronted.

'Well?' she said, staring hard at the crown of his bent head.

It took him a few moments to realise he was being addressed.

'Well what?' he replied, puzzled.

'Have you any comment to make about the dinner?'

'Oh, it's nice,' he mumbled back.

'Is that it? Do I have to ask for compliments? And what about the casserole potatoes? What do you think of them?'

'Well – they're a bit soggy.' This was Dad's reluctant appraisal.

We shuffled our feet uncomfortably.

Mum fumed. She couldn't contain her anger.

'That's you. I can't try one new thing. It's always the same. Just open your mind a bit, will you?'

'You asked for my bloody opinion and you got it!' Dad bellowed back across the table, slamming his cutlery down on the small uneaten mound of offending spud.

We hated Mum and Dad rowing, but that evening I thought it was a positive sign that they were fighting again; it meant life was returning to normal. The tiptoeing around Dad that had started months ago was over. He must be getting better. I was perversely happy to be witnessing this particular fight.

I knew from experience that it would go one of two ways. Dad would either storm off to the garage or his shed and they would continue it later when we were out of sight, if not earshot. Or they would suck it in, bury it down under the weight of their full stomachs, and let it settle and ferment into a potent and bitter elixir along with the hundreds of other unresolved conflicts, hurtful comments and slights of married life. On this occasion they both inhaled deeply. They didn't have the heart or the enthusiasm for a full-scale argument – perhaps they were just out of practice. A strong dose of tension had to be endured instead. We were forced to continue eating in strained silence. Scraping at my plate, it was only the thoughts of dessert that kept me rooted there.

Mum had still only eaten a third of her meal. The rest of us were finished. In awkward silence, with nothing else to do, we watched her eat. She felt pressure – from us, from herself, from some impossible ideal of the mother and wife she should be – to get our dessert ready. We couldn't possibly be left waiting. And so she attempted to eat the remainder of her dinner and get dessert at the same time. She rushed around, removing the pudding from the oven to let it cool a little, filling the kettle with water to make tea, and snatching bites of her food.

Suddenly, there was a small gargling sound. It was a wet, shaky noise, and it was getting louder. I'd heard this noise before. I turned to look at Mum. She was leaning over the sink. Her face and neck were a deep red and there were purple blotches on her cheeks. She was choking. She kept her back to us but her struggle was visible through her stiffened torso and down into her rigid arms and hands as she clawed the edge of the sink.

I was frozen to the spot. I looked at Dad. He didn't seem concerned enough. Even though this had happened many times before, it filled me with fresh horror each time. I didn't think it was right that Dad sat at the table, still, with a detached look on his face, even if they had just had an argument.

Then Mum made a most terrible hacking noise from the back of her throat.

'Dad!' I pleaded, but it was too late. Catherine was on her feet and jumped across the kitchen to Mum, still shaking over the sink.

'D'you wanna drink of water?' she asked in an almost nurse-like tone.

Mum shook her head. I could see tears at the corner of her eyes. She pointed to her back; she wanted to be hit.

Catherine started gently, but with increasing force, she

walloped Mum between the shoulder blades. No one else in the room made a sound as Catherine dealt blow after blow.

Then there was a loud cough full of air, followed by a plop, as a piece of gristle from the ham landed in the dish water in the sink. Just as quickly as it had started, it ended. Mum's back began to relax as she at last caught her breath. She took a glass of water from Catherine and wiped her eyes.

'You okay?' Dad feebly asked.

Mum turned around and gave him a look that said it all. 'No thanks to you.'

She sat down at the table and in silence Catherine gathered our plates and piled them by the sink. She carried over the dish of rice pudding and our dessert bowls and placed them in front of Mum, who methodically served out five equal portions. Then she stood up and, with her back to us, started to wash the dishes.

Epilogue

I open the door and greet them with a wide smile. They beam back in return. Dad puts his walking stick in front of him and hoists himself into the hallway. Mum steps in gingerly after him. I help them take off their coats and direct them into the kitchen. Before we move from the hall, Mum hands over a bottle of chilled white wine and a freshly baked, still warm apple tart. The sugar has only been dusted on it moments before; it has not yet dissolved into the golden pastry. 'That's just a little something for yourselves,' she says. It smells sweet and buttery. I will put it aside for later.

We enter the kitchen and as soon as Dad is seated, I plonk the baby into his arms. She nuzzles against his big belly and gurgles and coos happily. The two of them openly relish each other's company, placed as they are at the two extreme ends of our family's lifecycle. I place a plastic bowl of mashed vegetables in front of Dad and ask him to feed her.

I offer wine to Mum and place a glass of fizzy orange at Dad's elbow. Then I finish the potatoes and take the beef and Guinness stew – always a popular dish – out of the oven for a final stir. Everything is ready. But there is enough time for me to sit down and relax for a few moments before serving dinner. I try to talk to Mum but she and Dad are completely occupied with their little granddaughter. Maybe when we're at the table we'll get to chat.

I serve up this heart-warming and utterly satisfying meal that I know will please three generations of my family's taste buds – I even add a little to the baby's bowl. I leave only a smear of mashed potato and a trickle of the gravy from the stew on my plate. I look around the table and each plate is as clean as mine. I am happy in my role now, sandwiched as I am between my parents and my child. I stand and gather the dirty plates and return to the kitchen to get the dessert. Chocolate and pear pudding – made with Mum and Dad's sweet tooth in mind. I bring the dessert to the table and serve it under my parents' eager gaze. I scoop some soft ice cream on the side. Silence descends on the table. I smile, sip my wine and drink it all in.